Historic Pub Crawls through New York

Manhattan

First Edition

Thomas J. Vosper

*To everyone that has joined me on pub crawls,
and everyone still to do so.*

About this book

Having spent the last 16 years arranging pub crawls with my friends and family, this book is a tribute to the locations and pubs that I have personally visited.

Whilst every effort has been made to ensure its accuracy at the time of print, there may be subsequent name changes or, worse, a pub may have ceased trading.

Every route includes at least 10 pubs and New York, more than most cities I have visited, tends to be 'flexible' on their opening times.

There are always more pubs to visit and, whilst I try and share the most interesting places (with the best beer), each route is planned more for the enjoyment of an entire route that covers an interesting area.

I have not made any commercial agreements to endorse any of pubs over another and sadly we miss out, or walk past, great pubs all the time - usually just to ensure we space out the route to sufficiently sober up between pubs.

This book has no rules and is merely a guide for you to explore the area and pubs within. If you pass a pub that looks good, then pop in – you never know what you might find!

Historic Pub Crawls through New York

10 Guided walks around Manhattan's iconic pubs and landmarks

"start spreading the news"

Contents

Preface

In the first few months, after publishing my first book, it has been a delight to share the pubs and the stories from the books on social media and I have been humbled by the suggestions to visit across the planet.

Most amazing has been to hear from the landlords and landlady's who have seen hundreds of new visitors, with a book in hand, exploring the city.

My first book was primarily focused around the tiny 'City of London' area, with the second casting its net further afield to the banks of the River Thames at Richmond and Putney and to the vast open spaces of Highgate Cemetery and Hampstead Heath.

After launching my experiences of re-visiting all the pubs in my books across social media, I was overwhelmed with the ideas and requests to explore even further afield.

Whilst I look forward to building and exploring routes around Scotland, the North West of England, Yorkshire and beyond over the next 12 months or so, I was always drawn across the ocean to discover the hidden gems of the concrete jungle that is New York City.

When I first thought of exploring routes around the straight lines and tall buildings, I cast my mind back to the many years I have visited Manhattan for my 'day job' in the past.

I would walk for what felt like miles around the vast exhibition halls of the ginormous Javits Centre, before heading out across Manhattan, by foot, to put in even more steps around this walkable city.

Having preferred to avoid the subway, I have found myself keen to walk around the city always with a dive bar, taverns, or sports bar to rest my weary feet.

I have been lucky to receive a warm welcome wherever I have gone, and always found something enjoyable on tap (or at least sufficient to quell the burning fire of Buffalo Chicken Wings with extra hot sauce).

'Historic' can have different meanings but, to me, I have always enjoyed exploring off the beaten track. A pub can be hundreds of years old or it can be around the corner, and the perfect place to stop, to one of the city's most iconic landmarks.

Whilst New York City has a significantly shorter recent history than I am used to in London, I find it is all relative and there is still a rich tapestry of neighbourhoods, landmarks and stories to explore across the city.

Some of the world's most recognisable landmarks exist in New York, from the iconic Statue of Liberty to the Empire State Building, the Flat Iron or The Crysler Building.

Even for relatively new constructions, by European standards, such as Moynihan Train Station or the Public Library it is hard to fathom how they would have appeared amongst the trams or horse and carriages of days gone by.

There is so much, just around Manhattan, to explore along the avenues, from the basement bars to the impressive high-rise buildings. And, always, there is always a pub or a bar with regulars happy to share tales of the city.

The biggest challenges when writing this book, was to use 'er' instead of 're' at the end 'centre' and also coping with the variable opening times of all the bars and venues.

As with my other books, the total routes are typically around a couple of miles, with a total walk time of around an hour and the gap between pubs often being 5-10 minutes, allowing for sufficient fresh air and recovery to maintain the energy and thirst for the next pint.

Many of the best times in life are spent laughing over a beer with friends, so I am honoured to explore the globe and share even more fascinating pubs showcasing some of the most iconic locations across this iconic city along the most delightful routes.

Hopefully you will enjoy these routes, and the pubs along them, with friends and family, as much as I have.

Manhattan

Geographically the smallest of the five New York City boroughs, Manhattan is the most densely populated and serves as its economic and administrative centre.

European settlements, in the originally Lenape territory, began with Dutch colonists in 1624 – originally named New Amsterdam.

When the trading post came under English control in 1664 it was renamed New York when King Charles II granted the lands to his brother – the Duke of York.

Situated on one of the world's largest natural harbours, New York (in the current Manhattan location) has held significant culture and strategic importance.

It was the nations capital for five years until 1790, and The Statue of Liberty has become a symbol of optimise and the US ideals as it has welcomed millions of immigrants since the end of the 19th Century.

It is Manhattan that is most closely associated with New York City by non-residents.

Anchored by Wall Street, in the Financial District, York City has been labelled both the most economically powerful city and the leading financial centre of the world.

Manhattan hosts the world's two largest stock exchanges by total market capitalization, the New York Stock Exchange (NYSE) and Nasdaq.

Its several airports rank amongst the busiest in the world, with Penn Station the busiest transportation hub in the Western Hemisphere.

The New York City Subway is the largest subway system in the world by number of stations and it links every borough except Staten Island. Of the 472 total stations, 151 are in Manhattan.

Its iconic skyline features the likes of the Empire State Building, the Chrysler Building and One World Trade Center that are now joined by the pencil-thin skyscrapers of Billionaires row (overlooking Central Park) and new developments such as Hudson Yards.

Its unique geology of underlying bedrock, known as the Manhattan schist, provides an ideal foundation for its skyscrapers.

But for a gap between 1894 and 1908, the world's tallest building resided continually in Manhattan involving eight different buildings holding the title.

Such structures, like the Equitable Building of 1915 which rises vertically forty stories from the sidewalk, prompted the passing of the Zoning Resolution in 1916 which required new buildings to contain setbacks withdrawing progressively from the street as they rose, to preserve a view of the sky at street level.

Based around the Flatiron district, the term Silicon Alley was coined to describe the area of tech companies located here in the 1990s during the dot-com boom - a nod to California's Silicon Valley.

The term has grown somewhat obsolete since 2003 as New York tech companies spread outside of Manhattan.

Manhattan is host to three tourist attractions that consistently appear in lists of the most visited, such as Times Square, Central Park, and Grand Central Station, amongst which are many multinational media conglomerates and the Headquarters for the United Nations.

Broadway consists of 41 professional theatres that seat 500+ and, along with London's West End, represent the highest commercial level of life performances is the English-speaking world.

It is the epicentre of LGBT sociopolitical ecosystem and is acclaimed as the cradle of the modern LGBTQ rights movement. The 1969 Stonewall Riots in Greenwich Village are widely considered to constitute the single most important event leading to the gay liberation movement.

The annual Pride March travels south along Fifth Avenue and is the largest pride parade in the world, attracting tens of thousands of participants and millions of spectators, on the sidewalk, each June.

Other notable parades include the world's oldest St. Patrick's Day Parade, the Greenwich Village Halloween Parade, Macy's Thanksgiving Day Parade and numerous ones commemorating the independence days of various nations – such as Philippine Independence Day Parade which is the largest outside Manilla.

The iconic Madison Square Gardens is home to both NBA team, The Knicks, and NHL's Rangers.

Manhattan is one of the highest-income locations in the US but, as of 2023, its cost of living is also the highest in the country.

The real estate market for luxury housing continues to be among the most expensive in the world, with Manhattan having the highest sale price per square foot in the United States.

The city is represented in several prominent idioms.

The phrase *'New York minute'* is meant to convey an extremely short time or instant; the expression *'Melting Pot'* was first coined to describe the densely populated immigrant neighbourhoods on the Lower East Side.

The Flatiron Building is said to have been the source of the phrase *"23 skidoo"* which is what cops would shout at men who tried to get glimpses under women's dresses being blown up by gusts of wind created by the unusual shape of the triangular building.

The most iconic idiom, *'The Big Apple'* dates back to the 1920s, when a reporter heard the term being used by New Orleans stable hands in reference to New York City's horse racetracks and subsequently named his racing column *'Around The Big Apple'*.

Prohibition

As a Londoner, exploring hundreds of years of history through pubs, it is easy to lose sight of the fact that, less than 100 years ago, the US banned the sale of alcohol and drove the thriving industry into speakeasies, bootlegging and crime syndicates.

When the Eighteenth Amendment passed in 1919 and was ratified by 46 out of 48 states it enabled legislation, known as the Volstead Act, that set down the rules for enforcing the federal ban and defined the types of alcoholic beverages that were prohibited.

This commenced a period from 1920 to 1933 where constitutional law prohibited the production, importation, transportation, and sale of alcoholic beverages which, at the time, it was the 5th largest industry in the United States.

Almost immediately after the Eighteenth Amendment became law, bootlegging became widespread. In just the first six months of 1920, the federal government opened 7,291 cases of violations and, in the first full year, the number of cases jumped to 29,114 violations and would continue rise dramatically over the next thirteen years.

Just five years in, by 1925, there were anywhere from 30,000 to 100,000 speakeasy clubs in New York City alone.

It is difficult to draw historic conclusions on the impact of Prohibition on the national levels of crime, as national records at the time were poor.

Organized crime was a major benefactor from Prohibition as, beforehand, Mafia groups and other criminal organizations had mostly limited their activities to prostitution, gambling, and theft.

From 1920, organized rum-running or bootlegging emerged in response to Prohibition which created a profitable, and sadly often violent, black market for alcohol sales.

By the late 1920s, opposition to Prohibition began to emerge nationwide. Whilst prohibition appeared to be successful in reducing death rates, admissions to state mental health hospitals, arrests for public drunkenness, and rates of absenteeism, opponents of the act claimed it stimulated the proliferation of rampant underground, organized and widespread criminal activity.

Prohibition created a huge black market that directly competed with a formal economy that was coming under increasing pressure due to the Great Depression.

Along with other economic effects, enforcing Prohibition caused a massive increase in costs and resources. During the 1920s the annual budget of the Bureau of Prohibition went up from $4.4m to a whopping $13.4m. On top of this, the U.S. Coast Guard spent around $13m annually on enforcing of prohibition laws and preventing smuggling.

State governments desperately needed the tax revenue alcohol sales had previously generated. Franklin Roosevelt was elected, in 1932, largely based on his promise to end prohibition.

This led to the Twenty-first Amendment that ended Prohibition, which to date, is the only time in American history a constitutional amendment was passed for the purpose of repealing another.

Upon repeal of national prohibition, it continued in 18 states, with the last state, Mississippi, finally ending it in 1966.

However, almost two-thirds of all states adopted some form of local option which enabled residents to vote for local prohibition if desired.

In more recent time, there are still numerous dry counties across the US that restrict or prohibit liquor sales.

Moore County, the home of whiskey producer Jack Daniel's, in Tennessee, is a dry county and so the product is not available at local stores or restaurants.

How to use this guide

Each route starts near a Subway Station, with walking directions shown side-by-side a numbered map corresponding to each pub. The NYC Metro has different entrances and exits depending on where you are traveling from – so the addresses of all venues are provided.

Throughout the directions, areas of interest, landmarks or facts are lettered against the corresponding details in the pages that follow.

There are also some images of things to look out for on each route, at the end of each section.

This book is designed to fit in you back pocket and be easy to carry as you explore the routes.

Should you wish to skip any pubs, or find your own route, then full pub details are provided for you to plot your own path. I have marked a couple of highlights for each route.

Often the routes have a few pubs condensed into a short distance, enabling you to curate your own smaller path.

New York is a city that never sleeps and many of the pubs open late afternoon midweek so, where required, I have provided alternative timings on their weekend hours. Sometimes, pubs may vary their opening hours.

Timings are provided as a guide, to ensure you can complete the route before late evening.

Historic Pub Crawls through New York

Manhattan

First Edition

Flatiron to Empire State

This short walk passes the iconic Flatiron building, before taking in the legendary Madison Square Park before heading on past the famous venue that it lent its name to.

After visiting some family-owned Irish pubs, around NoMad, the route finishes under the watchful gaze of the awe-inspiring Empire State Building.

It provides the perfect route, to pass some landmark locations, that encapsulate the picture-perfect postcard of NYC.

Highlights of the route are Mustang Harry's next to MSG that is always thriving during events, and Playwright next to Empire State Building.

Start at 18 Street Subway

1. Peter McManus Cafe   1:00pm
   152 7th Avenue, NY 10011

2. The Copper Still Chelsea   1:30pm
   206 7th Avenue, NY 10011

3. John Doe   2:30pm
   253 5th Avenue, NY 10016

4. Triple Crown Ale House   3:15pm
   330 7th Avenue, NY 10001

5. Mustang Harry's   4:00pm
   352 7th Avenue, NY 10001

6. Molly Wee   5:00pm
   402 8th Avenue, NY 10001

7. Tír na Nóg   5:45pm
   254 W 31st Street, NY 10001

8. Féile   5:30pm
   131 W 33rd Street, NY 10001

9. Legends   6:30pm
   6 W 33rd Street, NY 10001

10. The Playwright   7:30pm
    27 W 35th Street, NY 10018

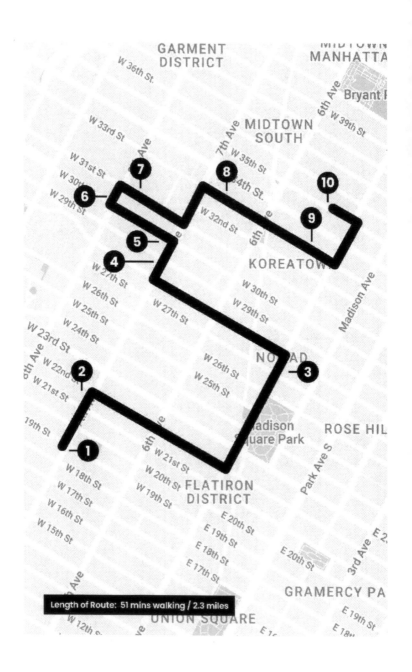

Length of Route: 51 mins walking / 2.3 miles

Directions

From the station, **Peter McManus Café (1)** is on 7th/West 19th Street. Continue past the pub on 19th Street and **The Copper Still (2)** is on the corner, a couple of blocks up.

Follow the traffic flow down 22nd Street before turning left onto 5th Avenue at Flatiron **(A)** past Madison Square Park **(B, C, D)** until reaching **John Doe (3)** on the corner of East 28th Street.

Head over the road, down West 28th Street, until turning right on 7th Avenue where **The Triple Crown Ale House (4)** is over the road, to the right, and **Mustang Harry's (5)** is the next block along 7th.

Turn left onto West 30th Street, where **Molly Wee (6)** is at the end of the block, before doubling back along 31st to **Tír na Nóg (7)** opposite Madison Square Gardens **(E)**.

Continue past the pub, before taking a left at 7th Avenue and turning onto West 33rd Street where **Féile (8)** is on the left.

Further along West 33rd Street, over 6th Avenue **(F, G)**, is **Legends (9)** in front of the Empire State Building **(G)**.

Pass the Empire State and turn left onto 5th Avenue, before taking a second left onto 35th where **The Playwright (10)** finishes the route.

1. Peter McManus Café

Opened in 1936, the Café is one of the oldest family-owned bars in the city. Alongside receiving several awards, it has appeared on film and television many times, including Highlander, The Other Guys, SNL, Seinfeld, Law & Order and many more.

Legend has it that there is a bullet hole, in a stained-glass cabinet, behind the bar.

2. The Copper Still

Listed in the top 10 whiskey bars in the country, with over 300 varieties behind the bar, this upscale bar only opened in 2014.

A. Flatiron Building

Originally named the Fuller Building, this 22-story, triangular construction was completed in 1902.

The name derives from its unusual shape and when it was built it was the tallest building in the city that was north of the financial district.

Inside, the most coveted offices sit at the 'point' of the building and include direct northern views of the iconic Empire State Building.

In popular culture, it has been used as the HQ for the Daily Bugle in the Spiderman trilogy and the location of April O'Neil's Channel 6 News in Teenage Mutant Ninja Turtles.

B. Madison Square Park

Although best known for providing the name of the famous sports arena which was located just northeast of the park for until 1925, the area was originally a swampy hunting ground that first came into use as a public space in 1686.

After various uses such as a baseball ground, a barracks and a children's home, it was opened as an official park, to the public, in May 1847 and was named after President James Madison.

In 1863, during the draft riots, over 10,000 troops descended on the square to control the rioters. Along with nearby Washington Square, it was also the site of a political rally, in support of the presidential candidacy of Democrat General George B. McClellan, who was running against Abraham Lincoln in 1864.

The park has a history of construction of ceremonial arches, in 1889 two temporary arches were built to celebrate the centenary of George Washington's first inauguration and just ten years later, in honour of Admiral George Dewey, the Dewey Arch was erected.

In 1918, $80,000 was spent to construct a Victory Arch to commemorate the city's war dead, however this too was dismantled at a later date.

C. National Museum of Mathematics (MoMath)
The first museum in the US to be dedicated to Maths was opened in 2012.

Its most famous exhibit is an unusual tricycle with square wheels, which operates smoothly on a catenary (curved such as a hanging chain) surface.

D. Museum of Sex (MoSex)

Located on the corner of East 27th Street, the museum focuses on a variety of subcultures and preferences such as lesbian and gay history and erotica, BDSM, pornography, and sex work - presented in an educational format.

It opened in 2002, and began an expansion project (including moving its entrance onto 5th Avenue) in 2009.

3. John Doe

Along with Jane Doe, the US and UK commonly uses these as placeholder names when the true identity is either unknown or deliberately concealed.

It is also commonly used in US law enforcement to refer to an unknown or unidentified corpse.

Variants include Richard/Jane Roe, John/Jane Smith, John/Jane Bloggs or just Baby Doe for children.

They have been used as placeholder names in many high-profile legal cases such as Roe v Wade or Doe v Bolton.

6. Molly Wee

In Irish, Mullagh Baíu means *"yellow hill"* and this pub gets its name from the location of the Reilly family home and farm located in County Cavan, 14 miles west of Cavan Town.

7. Tír na Nóg

Best known from the tale of Oisín and Niamh, Tír na nÓg is known as the 'Land of the Young' in Irish Mythology and is one of the names of the Celtic Otherworld.

It is depicted as an island paradise of everlasting youth, beauty, health, abundance, and joy and described as a beautiful place but dangerous or hostile to human visitors.

In the mythological tale, Oisín (a human hero) and Niamh (a woman of the Otherworld) fall in love so she brings him to Tír na nÓg on a magical horse that can travel over water.

After spending what feels like three years there, Oisín becomes homesick and longs to return home to Ireland.

Reluctantly agreeing, Niamh, lets him return on the magical horse, but warns him never to touch the ground. Upon returning, he finds that 300 years have passed in Ireland.

After accidentally falling from the horse, Oisín instantly becomes elderly, and he quickly dies of old age.

E. Madison Square Gardens

Opened in 1968, it is one of the business music arenas in the world and cost approximately $1.1Bn to construct – making it amongst the most expensive stadiums ever built.

Based between 7th and 8th Avenues, it forms part of the Pennsylvania Plaza which includes office and retail space including the train station.

In a controversial move, on expiry, its 10-year lease was renewed for only 5-years in 2023 and it is seen as an obstacle in the future development of Penn Station - which has relied on the opening of Moynihan Train Hall at the James Farley Post Office to expand in 2021.

F. Greeley Park Square

Named after Horace Greeley, who launched the New York Tribune in 1841, and held enormous influence on American popular opinion.

He ran for President in 1872, and was an advocate for protectionism, abolitionism, labour-rights, and political reform, with his famous advice *"Go West, young man, go West"* inspiring generations of Americans to seek their fortune in the new lands.

G. Jack Dempsey

Born William Harrison Dempsey in 1895, *"Jack"* was a professional boxer who reigned as the world heavyweight champion from 1919 to 1926.

Nicknamed Kid Blackie and The Manassa Mauler, he became a cultural icon of the 1920's due to his all-action fighting style and knockout power. Constant attached was viewed as his strategic defence.

A boxing Hall of Famer, he is ranked in the Top 10 of The Ring Magazines all-time heavyweights.

Sometimes surrounded by controversy, after his 1919 title fight against 6'6" Pottawattamie Giant, Jess Williard, he was accused of using loaded gloves, with wraps covered in plaster of Paris. Although since dismissed, rumours linger that he was using a knuckleduster.

One famous fight, known as The Long Count, was the first in entertainment history to draw a $2m gate which would be the equivalent of ~$50m is current times.

The fight itself was a 10-round rematch, with Gene Tunney, for the World Heavyweight Championship that took place in September 1926.

It was the first under the new knockdown rules, allowing fighters 10-seocnds to recover. Despite dominating the first half of the fight, in round seven, in front of the 104,843 in attendance, Gene Tunney was floored for the first time in his career.

Despite referee Dave Barry's instructions to return to a neutral corner, Dempsey, who often stood over downed opponents, looked down on Tunney for some time which provided his opponent precious seconds to recuperate.

On review a clock was superimposed that recorded Tunney's time on the floor as 13 seconds. After Tunney ended up winning, much has been debated to this day on whether allowing the count to start earlier would have seen Dempsey reclaim the title.

After receiving criticism for not enlisting for WWI - albeit a jury later exonerated him of draft evasion - Dempsey joined the New York State Guard but resigned to accept a commission as a lieutenant in the Coast Guard Reserve at the start of WWII.

To support the ongoing war effort, he made personal appearances at fights, camps, and hospitals before being promoted to commander in March 1944.

He was on board the attack transport USS Arthur Middleton, in 1945, for the invasion of Okinawa before receiving an honourable discharge from the Coast Guard Reserve in 1952.

9. Legends

Hosting The Football Factory, this popular sports bar hosts over 30 different supporters' groups and boasts the largest collection of football memorabilia in the US.

It shows live coverage of the English Premier League, the Football League, Bundesliga, Ligue 1, La Liga, Serie A, Major League Soccer, top South American leagues, and ALL UEFA Championships League and Europa League matches.

H. Empire State Building

The iconic, 102-story, Art Deco skyscraper is the amongst the tallest buildings in New York and was completed on 1st May 1931.

Each year around 4m tourists visit its observation decks, and it has become a cultural icon, both for its striking appearance and its inclusion in more than 250 films and television shows since King Kong was initially released in 1933.

It appears in the Seven Wonders of the Modern World by the American Society of Civil Engineers and ranks highly on many 'best of' lists for architecture and civil engineering.

Atop the 102nd story is the 203 ft pinnacle, mostly covered by broadcast antennas, and completed with a lightning rod.

The original intention of the Bethlehem Engineering Corporation was to build a 25-story office building on the site, with the company's president, Floyd De L. Brown, providing $100,000 of the $1m down payment required to start construction on the building. However, after defaulting on the loan and failing to secure additional funding the land was resold to Empire State Inc.

Plans became grander and after the original plan of the building was 50 stories, it was later increased to 60 and then 80 stories.

Height restrictions were placed on nearby buildings to ensure that the top fifty floors of the planned 80-story building would have unobstructed views of the city.

At 1,050 ft the new designs for The Empire State Building meant it would only be 4 feet taller than the Chrysler Building which was under construction and vying for the title of the world's tallest building.

With designers afraid that Chrysler might try to *"pull a trick like hiding a rod in the spire and then sticking it up at the last minute."*, plans were revised at the end of 1929, to include a 200 ft metal crown and an additional 222 ft mooring mast intended for blimps.

With the total roof height now 1,250 feet it meant the new design was the tallest building in the world by far when it was completed, just 18 months after the start of construction.

The construction phases of the Flatiron Building (above) showing its unusually shaped steel frame. The Square wheeled Tricycles (below) of MoMath.

In an attempt to raise funds for building the pedestal of the Statue of Liberty, its arm and torch (above) where exhibited in Madison Square Park from 1876 to 1882 – following a large celebration in honour of the centennial of the signing of the Declaration of Independence.

MSG (above) is home to the New York Knickerbockers – more commonly known as The Knicks. Alongside the Boston Celtics, the Knicks are one of two original NBA teams still located in its original city. Iconic World Heavyweight Champion Jack Dempsey mock punching Harry Houdini (below) who is being held back by fellow boxer Benny Leonard. Like Dempsey, Manhattan born Leonard is often revered amongst the top-rated boxers of all time. He fought an astonishing 219 times and held the lightweight Championship for 8 years until 1925.

The 86th floor observatory contains both an enclosed viewing gallery and an open-air outdoor viewing area (above), allowing for it to remain open 365 days a year. One of the city's most popular tourist spots there are five lines to enter the observation decks: the sidewalk line, the lobby elevator line, the ticket purchase line, the second elevator line, and the line to get off the elevator and onto the observation deck.

Greenwich to East Village

This delightful route, travels through the eclectic area of Greenwich Village and the 'Friends Apartment' and past some old Irish bars and bistros, before heading into the iconic Washington Square Park through Ukrainian Village and ending overlooking Tompkins Square Park in East Village

This route is ideal to experience one of NYC's most famous historic pubs alongside some truly unique locations.

McSorley's is probably the most famous pub in Manhattan and The White Horse Tavern is one of the oldest with a rich history serving writers and artists.

Start from 14 Street/8th Avenue Subway

1. Hudson Hound   1:00pm/4:00pm
   575 Hudson Street, NY 10014

2. White Horse Tavern   1:30pm/4:30pm
   567 Hudson Street, NY 10014

3. Galway Hooker Bar   2:15pm/5:15pm
   133 7th Ave Street, NY 10014

4. Arthur's Tavern   3:00pm/6:00pm
   57 Grove Street, NY 10014

5. The Village Tavern   3:30pm/6:30pm
   46 Bedford Street, NY 10014

6. Pubkey.bar   4:15pm/7:15pm
   85 Washington Place, NY 10011

7. Amity Hall Downtown   5:00pm/8:00pm
   80 W 3rd Street, NY 10012

8. Josie Woods Pub   5:45pm/8:45pm
   11 Waverly Place, NY 10003

9. McSorley's Old Ale House   6:30pm/9:30pm
   15 E 7th Street, NY 10003

10. The Grafton   7:30pm/10:30pm
    126 1st Avenue, NY 10009

11. St. Dymphna's   8:30pm/11:30pm
    117 Avenue A, NY 10009

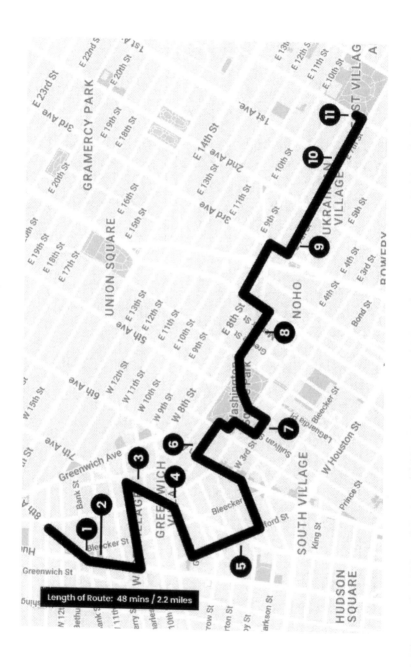

Length of Route: 48 mins / 2.2 miles

Directions

Exit station and head south on 8th Avenue, past the Museum of Illusions (**A**) and stay right at Jackson Square (**B**). As the road curves left there is **Hudson Hound (1)** with **White Horse Tavern (2)** a few doors down.

Continue past the pub, taking a second left onto Charles Street and turning right at 7th Avenue with **Galway Hooker Bar (3)** over the road. Exit the pub left and cross the major junction before crossing over at the Stonewall Monument Park (**C**), onto Grove Street where **Arthur's Tavern (4)** sits on the corner.

Head past the pub, over Bleeker Street (**D**), take a left at 'Friends Apartment' (**E**) onto Bedford Street and continue over 7th Avenue to **The Village (5)** before turning left onto Carmine Street (**F**).

At the end of the road (**G, H**), turn left onto 6th Avenue, before crossing and heading down West Washington Place. **Pubkey (6)** is hidden in a basement at the start of the road.

Continue to Washington Square (**I, J, K**) before turning right at the middle and heading one block to **Amity Hall (7)** on West 3rd Street.

Retrace back to the square, and cross to the far-right corner before heading away from the park down Waverly Place with **Josie Woods Pub (8)** on the corner.

Past the pub, turn left onto Broadway (**L**) before taking he second right on East 8th Street past The Astor Place Cube (**M**). At the next block, turn right onto 3rd Avenue with **McSorley's (9)** on East 7th Street.

Continue two blocks to **The Grafton (10)** on 1st Avenue, before continuing down East 7th Street to find **St. Dymphna's (11)** on Avenue A.

A. Museum of Illusions

This unusual exhibition is actually part of a franchise and claims to be the largest and fastest-growing chain of privately owned museums in the world with over 40 locations in over 25 countries.

With the NYC edition housed in a former banking house, it includes exhibits such as an infinity room and Ames room and various holograms and 3D art.

B. Jackson Square

One of the city's oldest parks, its triangular shape emerged from two footpaths in what is today's Meatpacking district and West Village. By the late 18th century, the footpaths had evolved into roads.

The First war memorial in the city was erected just a few hundred feet north of here, in 1762, and was an obelisk in honour of British Major General James Wolfe who died in the Battle of Quebec.

Although 1950's newspaper articles refer to 'Jackson Square' it is not clear when it formally adopted this name.

1. Hudson Hound

This modern Irish bar, overlooking Bleecker playground, claims to serve one of the best pints of Guinness on the East Coast.

2. White Horse Tavern

The second oldest continuously run tavern in NYC, since 1880, it was originally a longshoreman's bar catering to the workers from the nearby piers lining the Hudson River.

It gained its name from a once-popular brand of Scotch and built a reputation as a regular haunt for artists and writers from the nearby Greenwich Village. The most lauded of which, was Dylan Thomas, who was a regular in the 1950's.

Legend has it that Thomas drank his final drink here, before passing away in a nearby Chelsea hotel. Other famous patrons have included, James Baldwin, Bob Dylan, Jim Morrison and Hunter S. Thompson.

3. Galway Hooker Bar

Named after a type of traditional fishing boat, the Galway Hooker is a traditional Irish fishing boat common off the West Coast of Ireland.

Typically painted in pitch, its black appearance is striking with its dark red sails over a single mast with one mail sail. There are four classes of Irish Hooker boars, ranging from the smallest (The Leathbhád is about 28ft) to the largest (The Bád Mór is 44ft).

As Irish settlers moved to Boston, they built the hooker to cater to the fishing industry. As a result, these boats became known as 'Boston Hookers', 'Irish Cutters' or 'Paddy Boats'.

C. Stonewall Monument in Christopher Park

Sited in front of the famous Stonewall Inn, which was the birthplace of the Stonewall riots of 1969 and is widely considered to be the most important event leading to the Gay Liberation Movement and modern LGBTQ+ rights in the US.

The Stonewall National Monument is the first U.S. national monument dedicated to LGBT rights and was designated as a national monument President Barack Obama in 2016.

4. Arthur's Tavern

This historic building has hosted live Jazz and Blues bands since 1937. It was known for its fee admission in the 1970's and hosted The Chicagoans in the autumn of 1963.

D. Bleeker Street

Once a major centre for Bohemia (the cultural movement away from society's norms and expectations), it is named after the family farm the street ran through and is now popular for music and comedy venues

E. Friends Apartment

Amongst the most watched shows of all-time, this sitcom followed the lives of six friends in their 20's and early 30's and was mainly set in this Manhattan Apartment or the fictional café – Central Perk.

Despite the NYC setting, the filming actually took place in the Warner Bros. studios in Burbank California. It was met with some criticism for its depiction of financially struggling group of friends being able to afford what would be a hugely expensive apartment alongside the relatively hip setting of a coffee house.

The finale, aired in May 2004, was the fifth most-watched series finale in television history, only behind the finales of M*A*S*H, Cheers, The Fugitive, and Seinfeld. That year it was the second most-watched television broadcast in the US, only behind the Super Bowl.

5. The Village

Self-confessed 'drinking consultants' since 1998, this corner pub has an impressive long bar and a good selection of craft beers.

F. Carmine Street

This tree-lined, small street is famous both for its eateries and famous stores such as Carmine Street Guitars – which was subject to an award-winning documentary.

It is also the location of the famous Joe's Pizza which has run since 1975, and has featured in popular culture such as the Grand Theft Auto games; it was here where Peter Parker worked in Spiderman 2 and it also appeared on a food truck in Doctor Strange.

G. Our Lady of Pompeii Church

More formally known as the Shrine Church of Our Lady of Pompeii, this Catholic Church was founded in 1892 to serve the Italian-Americans who settled in Greenwich Village, and it has existed at its current location since 1926.

Del Gaudio's façade facing Carmine Street is built of limestone, with beige brick facing Bleecker Street. It cost over $1m to construct at the time - equivalent to $18m in 2023.

H. Father Demo Square

Renovated in 2007, the park is named after Father Antonio Demo, the former pastor of the neighbouring Our Lady of Pompeii Church from 1897 to 1935.

When the church was relocated to Carmine Street in 1928 it created the triangular plot of land that was improved to become this current public space.

6. Pubkey.bar (the Bitcoin Bar)

Ironically, bitcoin is the only payment this basement-level bar does not accept. Taken over from Crow's pub, the space has been occupied by various dives over the years and have now had a refresh with this Crypto theme bar.

The premises has a small recording studio that broadcasts live podcasts in front of the bar's patrons.

I. Alexander Lyman Holley Monument

Born in 1832, this American mechanical engineer was a founding member of the American Society of Mechanical Engineers and was considered the foremost steel and plant engineer and designer of his time. He made especially significant contributions in applying research to modern steel manufacturing processes.

Holley was a close friend of Zerah Colburn, a well-known locomotive engineer, the two travelled together on the maiden voyage of Isambard Kingdom Brunel's Great Eastern in 1860.

The monument in the park was unveiled in 1890.

J. Washington Square Park

One of the city's best known public spaces, and has been used as far back as the mid-17th century, when the land was farmed by the Dutch.

In 1826 the city bought the land and the square was laid out, levelled, and turned into the Washington Military Parade Ground.

By the 1830's the surrounding streets had become some of the city's most desirable residential locations.

Fast forward to modern times and the presence of street performers is one of the defining characteristics of the park.

K. Washington Square Arch

Designed in 1891, this large marble arch commemorates the centennial of George Washington's 1789 inauguration. It is adapted from the form of a Roman Triumphal Arch and is close in design to the 1st-century Arch of Titus, in Rome.

The iconography of the Arch centres on images of war and peace. On the frieze are 13 large stars and 42 small stars, interspersed with capital "W"s.

During the excavations human remains, in a coffin, were uncovered 10 feet below ground level, alongside and a gravestone dated 1803.

7. Amity Hall

The official home of Manchester City's branch of NYC supporters and has hosted many of the players on tour over the years.

As well as MCFC, they are a New York City FC partner pub and follow Carolina Panthers. This venue was named after the famous Amity Street that sits at the heart of the Greenwich Village.

8. Josie Woods Pub

Sporting an impressive 14 HD TV's and a jukebox this pub has a long history as a frat boy pub. It's a proper NYC style underground bar.

L. Broadway

This is the oldest north–south thoroughfare in New York City and runs for 13 miles through Manhattan, 2 miles through the Bronx and a further18 miles through the Westchester County municipalities.

It began as the Wickquasgeck trail - carved into the brush by its Native American inhabitants and snaking through swamps and rocks along the length of Manhattan Island.

In Manhattan is widely known as the heart of the American commercial theatrical industry, and is used as a metonym for it.

M. Astor Place Cube

Also known as Alamo or simply The Cube, this Cor-Ten steel structure weighs about 1,800 pounds and is 8 feet long on each side.

Installed in 1967, it was one of 25 temporary art installations that were intended to remain for a six-month period; however, residents successfully petitioned the city to keep the installation in place indefinitely.

9. McSorley's Old Ale House

The oldest Irish salon in NYC, having been opened in 1854, was one of the last 'Men only' pubs only admitting women when forced to do in 1970. The toilets became unisex and it wasn't until 1986 that a ladies washroom was installed.

Filled with memorabilia of 'Olde New York' that has remained on the walls since 1910 without change, it contains Harry Houdini's handcuffs connected to a bar rail.

Wishbones adorned the ceilings, which were hung by soldiers heading to WW1, with the remaining wishbones representing those that never returned.

The previous motto of 'Raw Onions and No ladies' has since been replaced with 'Be good or be gone' and there have been many notable patrons over the years including, John Lennon, Abraham Lincoln, Dustin Hoffman and Hunter S. Thompson.

11. St. Dymphna

Although often spelt many ways, the story of this 7th century Saint was first recorded in 13th century by a French canon of the Chrus of Aubert.

She was 14 when her mother died and her father was pressed to remarry someone as beautiful as his first wife.

She fled her home, on learning of her father's growing desire to marry her, given her resemblance to her deceased mother. After settling in Gheel, she built a hospice for the sick and mentally ill before being beheaded without reason some years later.

With her history of miraculous healings of the mentally ill, she was martyred by her father and is the patron for mental health professionals.

Greenwich Village (above) gets its name from Groenwijck which is Dutch for 'Green District.' The interior of Our Lady of Pompeii (below) is decorated in the Romanesque Revival style and lined with polished marble Corinthian columns.

The sculpture of George Washington as Commander-in-chief and President (above) appears on either side of the Washington Arch in Washington Square Park.

Founded in 1859, by American industrialist Peter Cooper, one of the richest people in the US, The Cooper Union is a private college for the advancement of Science and Art.

Born into a workingman's family, he had less than a year of formal schooling. Despite his upbringing, Cooper designed and built America's first steam railroad engine and made his fortune by owning both glue factory and an iron foundry.

He was a principal investor and initial president of the New York, Newfoundland and London Telegraph Company, which laid the first transatlantic telegraph cable. He was also the oldest person ever nominated for the office by a political party, when he ran for President under the Greenback Party.

During 2015 the Alamo was removed for renovation works, leading to an unknown man (above) dressing up as The Cube for Halloween. Under the watch of The Empire State Building, Tompkins Square Park (below) has benefitted from the gentrification of East Village, to become a regular spot for sun seekers and leisure activities.

The Bowery to Financial District

Starting amongst the eclectic street art of The Bowery, before passing the location for one of the silver-screens most iconic scenes, this route skirts the edge of Chinatown, under the landmark Manhattan and Brooklyn Bridges before heading through the old port.

Passing the Seaport and some of the oldest buildings of Lower Manhattan the route meanders through the famous financial district, over cobbled streets and provides a glimpse into 17th-century New Amsterdam.

The route is notable for finishing in the world-famous Dead Rabbit which was won numerous 'Best Bar' awards.

Start from Broadway-Lafayette Street Metro

1. Sláinte   1:00pm
    304 Bowery, NY 10012

2. Kelly's Sports Bar   1:45pm
    12 Avenue A, NY 10009

3. Clockwork Bar   2:30pm
    21 Essex Street, NY 10002

4. 169 Bar   3:15pm
    169 East Broadway, NY 10002

5. Mr. Fong's   4:00pm
    40 Market Street, NY 10002

6. Cowgirl Sea-Horse   5:00pm
    259 Front Street, NY 10038

7. Jeremy's Ale House   6:00pm
    228 Front Street, NY 10038

8. The Full Shilling   7:00pm
    160 Pearl Street #1, NY 10005

9. Ulysses or Stone St Tavern   8:00pm
    Stone Street, NY 10004

10. The Dead Rabbit   9:00pm
    30 Water Street, NY 10004

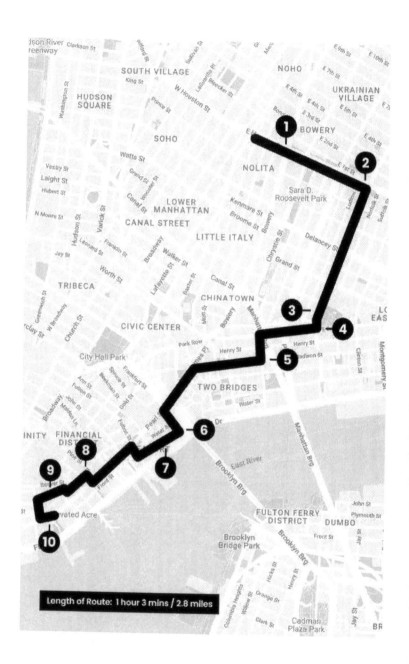

Length of Route: 1 hour 3 mins / 2.8 miles

Directions

Turn East out of the station, taking the left at Bowery Street (**A**) where **Sláinte (1)** is a few doors down. Heading back down East Houston Street (**B**), past First Street Green Park (**C**), and Katz Delicatessen (**D**), turn left onto Avenue A where **Kelly's Sports Bar (2)** is across the road.

Turn left from the pub and continue along what becomes Essex Street for about 15mins until reaching **Clockwork Bar (3)**, which is opposite Seward Park (**E**). **169 Bar (4)** is near the corner of the park on East Broadway.

Continue for some time along East Broadway, away from the park, at the edge of Chinatown (**F**) taking the first left onto Market Street after passing under Manhattan Bridge (**G**). **Mr. Fong's (5)** is on the corner at the end of the block.

Continue along Madison Street, following it left at St. James Place under Brooklyn Bridge (**H**)before taking the first left at Dover Street, adjacent to the Bridge. Two blocks down, on the corner is **Cowgirl Sea-Horse (6)**. Head along Front Street over the pedestrian area (**I**), to find **Jeremy's Ale House (7)** on the right.

Remain on Front Street, into the pedestrian zone, taking a first right at South Street Seaport Museum (**J**), before turning left at the Titanic Memorial Park (**K**), on Water Street. Three blocks over, turn right onto Pine Street, where **The Full Shilling (8)** is down the first left.

Turn left out of the pub, along Pearl Street (**L**), before turning right after the Queen Elizabeth II September 11th Garden (**M**) and taking a quick left onto the cobbled Stone Street where there is a choice of **Ulysses** or **Stone Street Tavern (9)**.

Continue past the pub to the junction, before turning left back then back onto Pearl Street and crossing at Portal Down to Old New York (**N**) and down Coenties Street, where **The Dead Rabbit (10)** is on the right.

A. The Bowery

The oldest thoroughfare on Manhattan Island, precedes even European intervention as it was originally a Lenape footpath spanning the entire length of the island.

As the Dutch settlers arrived, they named the path Bouwerie road - *'bouwerie'* being an old Dutch word for farm as it connected the farmlands and estates on the edge of the city into what is today's Wall Street and Battery Park area.

B. The Bowery Mural

This outdoor exhibition space has been owned by Goldman Properties since 1984, and is located on the corner of Houston Street and the Bowery.

Before coming under their ownership, it had become a popular graffiti spot, when street artist Keith Haring created a large mural here in 1982.

This icon capot has been used by many artists and institutions to draw attention to global issues, such as guns in America, a 2018 piece by Banksy highlighting the imprisonment of an artist by the Turkish government and Tomokazu Matsuyma's celebration of global culture in 2019.

Sadly, due to an increase in vandalism, in May 2022, the owners of the wall announced an indefinite break from commissioning new murals.

C. First Street Green Park

Hard to spot amongst the two tenement style apartment buildings, this art park is forever changing throughout its seven-plus years of existence.

Hosting between 25-32 murals at any one-time, aspiring artists can submit their designs to the parks' organisers before being selected to impart their design amongst the hedgerows.

D. Katz Delicatessen

Since its founding, it has been popular among locals and tourists alike for its pastrami on rye, which is widely considered among New York's best.

Each week, Katz's serves 6,800 kg of pastrami, 3,600 kg of corned beef, 910 kg of salami and over 4,000 hot dogs.

The deli has several catchphrases, notably *'Katz's, that's all!'* whose origin comes from a sign maker who asked the owners what to paint on the deli's sign. When the owner replied *'Katz's, that's all,'* it was misunderstood and painter verbatim by the sign maker, and it still stands today.

Although featured in many films and television shows, it is most famous as the site of Meg Ryan's fake orgasm in the 1989 romantic comedy 'When Harry Met Sally'.

In the scene featuring the two title characters having lunch, the couple are arguing about whether a man can recognize when a woman is faking an orgasm. Adamant that men cannot tell the difference, and to prove her point, Sally vividly fakes one as other diners watch.

As the scene ends with Sally casually returning to her meal, a nearby patron places her order, simply stating: *'I'll have what she's having.'* – a quote that was ranked 33rd in AFI's 100 years.... 100 Quotes list of the most memorable movie lines.

3. Kelly's Sports Bar

In the 1970's the surrounding area was notorious for drug crimes and gang conflict, and this bar is believed to be haunted following the murder of six people in the basement.

It's the only Buffalo Bills fan bar in NYC and proudly displays a football signed by Hall of Famer Thurman Thomas behind the bar.

E. Seward Park

Named after William Henry Seward, who was a senator in the mid-1800's that went on to be the Secretary of State and part of the Lincoln Administration.

Peculiarly it holds one of the few statues in the U.S. dedicated to Togo, who was the sled dog who was instrumental in the 1925 serum run to Nome in Alaska.

The Great Race of Mercy, was the transport of a diphtheria antitoxin across Alaska by 20 mushers and about 150 sled dogs. Together they covered over 674 miles (1,085 km) in just over 5 days and saved the small town of Nome and surrounding communities from a developing epidemic of diphtheria.

The mushers and their dogs were portrayed as heroes on radio and received headline coverage in newspapers across the US.

Balto, was the lead sled dog on the final stretch, and became the most famous canine celebrity of the era after Rin Tin Tin - is Central Park statue is a popular tourist attraction.

But the most dangerous parts of the route were covered by Togo's team as well as a greater distance of 261 miles compared to Balto's 55 miles.

In any case, the resulting fame led to an increased in inoculations and a dramatic reduction in the threat of the disease.

4. 169 Bar

Open since 1916, it was ordinally known as the Bloody Bucket and claims to be the home of the Pickle Martini.

Owned by New Orleans native, Charles Hanson, who took over in 2006, who initially came up to NYC in 1978 as one of the lead artists in Punk band 'The Normals'.

Despite a successful music career, that included spending 11 weeks on the Billboard Dance Charts, Charles started working as a bike messenger as training for semi-professional bicycle racing during the Lance Armstrong era.

After a messenger party one night, Charles was hit by a limo. While incapacitated with a broken knee and shoulder, he fostered the idea of becoming a professional and while subsequently working at the 169 Bar he had the opportunity arose to purchase the bar with the insurance money from the limo hit.

F. Chinatown

The first Chinese person to have arrived in the area, in the 1850's, is believed to be businessman Ah Ken, who founder a successful Cigar store on Park Row.

Soon after the California Gold Rush bought around 25,000 immigrants in search of the 'Gold Mountain' – although most found work as 'cigar men' or carrying billboards around town.

Legend has it that Ah Ken owned a small boarding house which housed the first immigrants to arrive in Chinatown, before funnelling his rental profits into his cigar store around which modern day Chinatown has been built.

Although historically, Chinatown was primarily populated by Cantonese speakers, the 1980-1990s saw large numbers of Fuzhounese-speaking immigrants arrive and form a sub-

neighbourhood which was annexed to the east of Chinatown and has since become known as Little Fuzhou.

G. Manhattan Bridge

One of four toll-free bridges connecting Manhattan Island to Long Island, it was opened to traffic on 31st December 1909.

Due to its innovative use of deflection theory for deck stiffening, it is considered the precursor of modern suspension bridges – and has been a model for many of the record-breaking spans in the early 20th-century from its first use of the weight-saving Warren truss.

The bridge has four vehicle lanes on the upper level, which is split between two roadways carrying traffic in opposite directions. The lower level has three Manhattan-bound vehicle lanes; four subway tracks; a walkway on the south; and a bikeway on the north.

5. Mr. Fong's

This trendy location, whilst aiming to be a neighbourhood bar, has become a hotspot for the fashion industry and regularly entertains a mix of Vogue editors and fashion models.

H. Brooklyn Bridge

At the time of opening, in 1883, this held the title of the longest suspension bridge in the world and was the first fixed crossing of the East River.

Over one million people paid to cross in the six first months, after opening. The bridge carried 8.5 million

people in its first full year of operation, before doubling to 17 million in 1885 and again to 34 million in 1889.

Whilst many crossing were cable car passengers, around 4.5 million pedestrians a year were crossing the bridge for free by 1892.

Since opening, the bridge has developed a reputation as a suicide bridge due to the number of jumpers who do so with the intention to kill themselves, though exact statistics are difficult to find.

The first known jumper to die was Robert Emmet Odlum - brother of women's rights activist Charlotte Odlum Smith - in 1885.

It is believed the first person to jump from the bridge with the intention of committing suicide was Francis McCarey in 1892.

Several notable feats have taken place on or around the bridge, such as when Giorgio Pessi piloted what was at the time one of the world's largest airplanes, the Caproni Ca5, under the bridge, in 1919.

I. Peck Slip

The Peck Slip Ferry was a pre-Brooklyn Bridge ferry route connecting Manhattan and Williamsburg in Brooklyn. It began operating in 1836 as a supplemental service to the Grand Street Ferry which was located a little further down on the site of the Old Fulton Fish Market.

7. Jeremy's Ale House

Occupying a former filet house on Front Street, it originally opened as a beer and sandwich shop in a flea market – now South Street Seaport Museum – in 1974.

In an attempt to drum up business during the early years the started offering women $25 for their bras, which he would then hang from the ceiling of the bar. This tactic led to crowds of hundreds at the weekend.

J. South Street Seaport Museum

South Street Seaport's historic area features some of the oldest buildings in Lower Manhattan. It was here that the first pier was constructed by Dutch settlers in 1625.

In 1728, the Schermerhorn Family established trade with South Carolina, which saw rice and indigo arrive from Charleston.

The port also became the focal point of delivery of goods from England, around the same time, but in 1776, during the American Revolutionary War, the British claimed the port, adversely affecting trade during its occupation.

When many traders returned to England, in 1783, most of port enterprises collapsed – before quickly recovering from the post-war crisis.

For many years, from 1797 until around the 1850's, New York had the country's largest system of maritime trade and the port was named the Port of New York.

On 22nd February 1784, the Empress of China sailed from Guangzhou bringing a cargo of green and black teas, porcelain, and other goods - marking the beginning of trade

relations between the newly formed United States and the Qing Empire.

In early 1818, the first regular trans-Atlantic voyage route, the Black Ball Line, opened when the 424-ton transatlantic packet James Monroe sailed from Liverpool.

Leading to the creation of many competing companies, such as the Red Star Line in 1822, the new shipping transportation significantly contributed to the establishment New York as one of the centres of world trade.

K. Titanic Memorial Park

The construction of this 60-ft lighthouse was instigated by Titanic survivor, Margaret Brown (also known as unsinkable Molly Brown) to remember the passengers and crew that lost their lives on 15th April 1912.

Featuring a Time Ball, the lighthouse was originally erected and formally dedicated in 1913, on the one-year anniversary of the sinking.

From 1913 to 1967, the time ball would be raised to the top of the rod on the lighthouse and dropped to signal twelve noon to ships in New York Harbour.

8. The Full Shilling

Although opened in 1999, the history of the pub is much older, with its 101-year-old bar being shipped directly from a Belfast pub.

In slang, it is often used in the negative sense to highlight a lack of control of an individual's mental faculties.

L. Pearl Street

This was one of the first and busiest streets in Lower Manhattan and gets its name for the variety of coastal pearl shells traded here.

Its unusual because of its irregular course which is due to it following the original eastern shoreline until the latter half of the 18th-century when years of landfill extended the shoreline approximately 200-300m further into the East River - first to what is now Water Street and then later to Front Street.

M. Queen Elizabeth II September 11th Garden

Whilst originally planned as The British Memorial Garden, it was officially renamed The British Garden at Hanover Square by Prince Harry in 2009.

Since it commemorates the Commonwealth of Nations member states' victims of the 9/11 attacks on the World Trade Center it was renamed the Queen Elizabeth II September 11th Garden at a rededication ceremony led by the Dean of Westminster Abbey in May 2012.

9. Ulysses, Underdog or Stone Street Tavern

Located on historic Stone Street, which one of New York's oldest streets, incorporating two 17th-century roads in the Dutch colony

It became the first cobbled street in New Amsterdam during 1658 and, despite being renamed Duke Street by the British, took back its original name in 1794.

The street contains several prominent structures, including 1 Hanover Square, which was the New York Cotton Exchange.

In the early 1990's much of the street was rundown and was purchased by developer Tony Goldman with the aim of bringing it back to its former glory.

Around the same time, the district was also added to the National Register of Historic Places and the LPC, city agencies, and Downtown Alliance collectively contributed $1.8 million toward its renovation and restoration work.

Old-style lampposts and ~23,000 cobblestones were installed with the work completed in 2000, turning the eastern section of Stone Street into a busy restaurant district over the following decade

N. Portal Down to Old New York

The Stadt Huys was the first city hall and was built by the Dutch in 1642. Long since demolished, the remnants along with those of former governor Francis Lovelace's house were discovered during the construction of 85 Broad Street, in 1979.

Along the sidewalk are several transparent panels are located, allowing insight into the original foundation walls can be observed.

10. The Dead Rabbit

Also known in full as 'The Dead Rabbit Grocery and Grog,' it was named the best bar in the world in 2016, despite only opening just three years earlier.

The five-storey, 19th-centruy townhouse splits across three distinctly different experiences: The Taproom, The Parlor, and the Occasional Room.

It is named after The Dead Rabbit gang – Irish immigrants who fought long and hard to defend their poverty-stricken slum back in the mid-1800s.

Formed to protect the immigrant Irish underclass against the Bowery Boys, The Dead Rabbits were also a criminal organization with extensive connections in New York politics.

When their leader, John Morrissey died in 1878, he had become an acclaimed businessman, congressman, and senator. Known for his skills as a bare-knuckle boxer, legend has it that the entire New York senate turned out for his funeral, just to be sure he was dead.

The conflict was dramatized in Martin Scorsese's Oscar winning motion picture 'Gangs of New York' in 2002 and the bar has the film props used by Liam Neeson in the fight scenes hanging on the downstairs wall.

The Barry McGee Mural (above) on the corner of Houston Street and The Bowery. His installations usually consist of simple bold designs, influenced by Islamic patterns on tiles. Depicted in the Disney+ moving of the same name, Togo (below) was a heroic dog during the 1925 Serum Run.

The main span of Manhattan Bridge, seen being constructed in 1909 (above) is 451m long, with the suspension cables being 983m long. With the bridge's total length is 2,089m.

At the Manhattan end of the bridge is a Beaux-Arts triumphal arch and colonnade (below) that was completed in 1915. Made of white, fine-grained Hallowell granite, the structures are decorated with two groups of allegorical sculptures and a frieze called *'Buffalo Hunt.'*

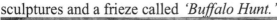

The Fulton Fish Market (above) cast a gloomy presence during the Great Depression. Standing on the roof of the Seaman's Church Institute (below) the Titanic Memorial Lighthouse would signal twelve noon to the harbour.

Constructed in 1854, 1 Hanover Square housed The New York Cotton Exchange, founded in 1870, between 1872 and 1885.

The building subsequently served as the headquarters of W.R. Grace and Company until the early 1910, before being purchased by the India House, in 1914, which is a private club for gentlemen involved in foreign commerce, and continues to occupy the building today.

Tribeca to The Battery

This historic route travels through some of the oldest parts of the city, on the edge of The Hudson, whilst catching more modern sights like 'The Ghostbusters' Fire Station.

The direct route skirts the iconic yet sombre 9/11 memorial and Freedom Tower before reaching the famous Battery Park and the edge of the Financial District, past the famous Wall Street Bull.

Particular highlights of this route are the intimate Ear Inn, which is one of New York's oldest bars; and the elegant Fraunces Tavern which deserves its place amongst some of Manhattan's oldest buildings.

Start from Houston Street Subway

1.	Ear Inn 326 Spring Street, NY 10013	2:00pm
2.	Greenwich Street Tavern 399 Greenwich Street, NY 10013	2:45pm
3.	Walkers 16 N Moore Street, NY 10013	3:15pm
4.	Puffy's Tavern 81 Hudson Street, NY 10013	3:45pm
5.	Mudville 9 126 Chambers Street, NY 10007	4:30pm
6.	Monk McGinns 57 Murray Street, NY 10007	5:15pm
7.	O'Hara's 120 Cedar Street, NY 10006	6:15pm
8.	Blarney Stone 11 Trinity Place, NY 10006	7:00pm
9.	White Horse Tavern 25 Bridge Street, NY 10004	7:45pm
10.	Fraunces Tavern 54 Pearl Street, NY 10004	8:30pm

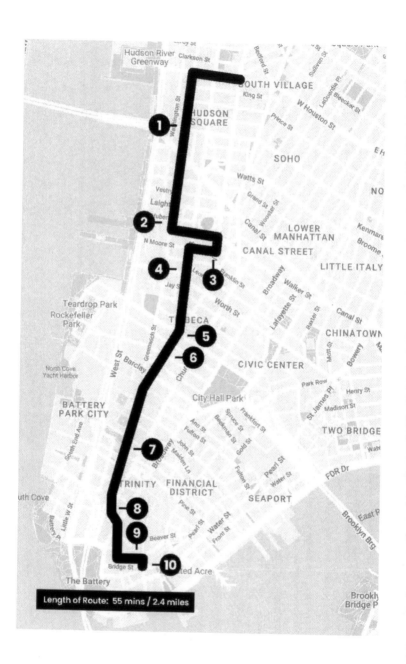

Length of Route: 55 mins / 2.4 miles

Directions

Exit the station **(A)** and head towards the river, taking the second left onto Greenwich Street where **Ear Inn (1)** is a couple of blocks down on Spring Street in James Brown House **(B)**. Continue South, along Greenwich Street **(C)**, where **Greenwich Street Tavern (2)** is a few blocks away.

Leave the pub along Beach Street and take a second Right onto Varick Street. The 'Ghostbusters HQ' **(D)** is on the corner with **Walker's (3)** opposite. Head away from the Fire Station, along North Moore Street, taking the first Left onto Hudson Street **(E)** where **Puffy's Tavern (4)** is a couple of blocks away.

Follow the road until it ends at West Broadway **(F)**, where **Mudville9 (5)** is over the road down Chambers Street. After retracing back to the main road, **Monk McGinn's (6)** is after the next block down Murray Street.

Follow the main road **(G)**, across the pedestrian areas and past the 9/11 memorials **(H, I, J)**. Continue onto Greenwich Street, with **O'Hara's (7)** past the memorial and opposite the Church grounds **(K)**.

Leave the pub along Cedar Street, turning left onto Trinity Place **(L)**. As the road curves right, **The Blarney Stone (8)** is hidden with its tiny frontage on the curve under the office blocks.

Take the first left, down Morris Street, before turning right past the Bronze Bull **(M)**, heading to the left on Broadway until Bridge Street, left at the far corner of the museum **(N, O)**.

The White Horse Tavern (9) is along this road with **Fraunces Tavern (10)** on the corner at the next junction.

A. Houston Street

Running the full width of Manhattan, this major thoroughfare generally acts as the boundary line between East Side Manhattan and The Lower East Side.

The street's name is pronounced "HOW-sten", which is different to the city of Houston, in Texas, whose name is pronounced "HYOO-sten".

Nikola Tesla established his laboratory here in 1891, however much of his research was lost in a fire just four years later.

The current spelling of the name is a corruption of the surname of William Houstoun from whom it gets its name. In fact, it appears as Houstoun in the city's Common Council minutes for 1808 and the official map that was drawn up three years later in 1811.

1. The Ear Inn

It gets its name from the famous broken neon sign outside, which was altered in the 70's when the owners covered the round parts to bypass a lengthy review of a new signage application.

This historic building was constructed in 1770, and during prohibition it was transformed into a speakeasy with the upstairs apartment hosting a mix of inhabitants from a doctor's surgery to a smugglers den to a brothel.

Legend has it that its downstairs bar has been haunted since 1833 by the ghost of a murdered sailor called Mickey.

B. James Brown House

This nationally listed building is one of the few existing examples of Federal architecture in New York.

The building's appearance was first recorded in 1817, and was originally the home of African-American Revolutionary War veteran, James Brown.

It would have only been a few feet from the Hudson River at the time of construction, however landfill and further developments have increased the distance.

Originally a tobacco store, it was likely turned into a bar earlier than 1835 making it one of the oldest taverns in New York.

Although sold in anticipation of the 1919 introduction of prohibition laws, bar re-opened afterwards, but now existed as a business without a name – simply called "The Green Door".

C. Greenwich Street

Running parallel to the Hudson River, it was the only continuous road from Lower Manhattan to Greenwich Village in the 1790's – other than Broadway.

By the early 19th century Greenwich Street became one of the most fashionable residential neighbourhoods in the city, but by the 1850's many of the wealthy residents had moved and made way for boarding houses, a wax museum, and John Bill Rickett's Equestrian Circus.

Edgar Allan Poe, the Poet and writer, was said to have lived in a boarding house on the street briefly between 1844 and 1845.

2. Greenwich Street Tavern

This busy sports bar was named in Gotham's 24 best pubs in NYC in 2023 and proudly claims to be The Original Home of the Buffalo Chicken Dip.

3. Walkers

This delightful pub, owned by the team behind Ear Inn, dates back to the 1880's and proudly displays one of its original licences. Over recently years it has been fully restored, removing the previous landlords attempts to cover the ornate ceiling and décor with a suspended ceiling and plain box work.

D. Ghostbusters HQ

This firehouse is home to Hook & Ladder Company 8 and is instantly recognisable for its appearance as the Headquarters in the Ghostbusters films.

Built in 1903, the building originally had two vehicle doors, but was halved in size during 1913 after Varick Street was widened.

As well as appearing in the 1984 comedy, it has made appearances in the film Hitch and TV series Seinfeld and How I Met Your Mother.

E. Hudson Street

Whilst there are many notable buildings along the street, it hosts the headquarters of radio station WQHT (also known as Hot 97) which was the site of a gunfight between entourages of 50 Cent and The Game in 2005.

It has also been home to several notable residents such as John Cheever, Jane Jacobs and Tiger Woods.

4. Puffy's Tavern

This old, laid-back 1940's era boozer serves a variety of Italian sandwiches alongside a selection of beers.

F. Bogardus Plaza

This volunteer-run open space is named after the renowned inventor and cast-iron architect – 19th-century pioneer James Bogardus.

It is the work of Bogardus that has led to the wide use of steel frame building construction that still used in modern-day skyscrapers.

6. Monk McGinn's

This multistorey craft beer bar is decorated in a 1920's style of high ceilings, exposed brick and exposed wood beams and piping throughout.

G. Silverstein Family Park

When the chairman of Silverstein Properties, Larry Silverstein, opened the original 7 World Trade Center in 1987, he and his wife filled the lobby with contemporary artwork, over following years.

In April 2001, he completed a $3.22Bn lease-purchase agreement for One, Two, Four, and Five World Trade Center.

The lease included the obligation to rebuild the structures if they were destroyed.

Following the 9/11 terrorist attacks, he became embroiled in a multi-year dispute with insurers over where the attacks has constituted one event, or two, before eventually settling with insurers agreeing to payout $4.55Bn.

Among his many real estate projects, he is the developer of the rebuilt World Trade Center complex, as well as one of New York's tallest residential towers at 30 Park Place.

H. One World Trade Center & September 11 Memorial

Formerly called the Freedom Tower, during initial planning and construction, it is the main building of the rebuilt World Trade Center following the destruction caused by the 9/11 terrorist attacks.

In the year following the attacks, Ground Zero became the most visited place in the US leading to plans quickly coming together to memorialize the September 11 attacks and rebuild the complex.

By 2002 the Lower Manhattan Development Corporation had organized a competition to determine how to redevelop the site.

Peter Walker and Michael Arad's *"Reflecting Absence"* proposal was selected as the site's 9/11 Memorial in January 2004, with the final design for the *"Freedom Tower"* formally unveiled on June 28, 2005.

The top floor of One World Trade Center is 1,368 feet above ground level, with a 33'4" parapet taking it to the identical roof height of the original One World Trade Center.

The Towers Spire is 1776 feet- which is intended to symbolize the signing of the United States Declaration of Independence in 1776.

I. The Survivor Tree

Found amongst the rubble, with its root and limbs snapped or damaged, this Callery pear tree was recovered from Ground Zero in the aftermath of the attacks and was nursed back to health, before being returned to the 9/11 Memorial Site in 2010.

J. FDNY Memorial Wall

Dedicated to the 343 members of the NYC Fire Department and Glenn J. Winuk, who was a volunteer firefighter, who lost their lives on 11th September 2001.

It spans the west exterior wall or FDNY Engine 10, Ladder 10 station.

7. O'Hara's Pub & Restaurant

Badly damaged, amongst the wreckage of 9/11, this pub became a haven for first responders and Ground Zero workers.

Opened in 1983, there are thousands of patches from firefighter uniforms throughout which started just over a year after the attack.

K. St. Nicholas Greek Orthodox Church

Replacing the original church, that was destroyed on 9/11, the church was consecrated on 4th July 2022.

Its architecture takes inspiration from Byzantine influences, most notably the Church of the Savior and the Hagia Sophia in Istanbul, and the Parthenon in Athens.

The original church was founded in 1916, with parishioners initially worshipping in the dining room of a hotel on Morris Street.

By 1919, five families had raised $25,000 to purchase a new location for the church, an 1830's three-story private home on 155 Cedar Street, that had been repurposed into a tavern. The modest structure was converted into a church by 1922.

L. Elizabeth H. Berger Plaza

Formerly known as the Edgar Street Greenstreet, this triangular park is named in honour of the civic advocate Elizabeth H. Berger who advocated for the fusion of two traffic triangles at this location into an expanded park.

The park is located on the site of a former bustling neighbourhood known as Little Syria which housed immigrants displaced by the construction of Brookly-Battery tunnel in 1953.

8. Blarney Stone

Built into the battlements of Blarney Castle, legend has it that kissing the stone blesses the kisser with the skill of flattery and great eloquence – also known as the gift of the gab.

The origin of the legend is unknown; however, one early story tells of the goddess Clíodhna. In the midst of an ongoing lawsuit, Cormac Laidir MacCarthy, the builder of Blarney Castle and on the advice of Clíodhna, kissed the first stone he found in the morning on his way to court.

After doing so, it is rumoured that he pleaded his case with great eloquence and won – leading observers to note that the Blarney Stone is said to impart *"the ability to deceive without offending"*.

M. The Charging Bull

Often referred to as the Bull of Wall Street, the 3,200kg, Bronze sculpture depicts the symbol of financial optimism and prosperity.

It was created in the wake of the 1987 Black Monday stock market crash, by Italian Artist Arturo Di Modica who

arrived with the Bull on the back of a truck, in December 1989, and left it outside the New York Stock Exchange Building.

The Charging Bull was created to inspire everyone who encountered it to carry on fighting through the hard times.

It soon became a major tourist attraction and is one of the most photographed artworks in the city. In addition to having their pictures taken by its head, many tourists pose at the back of the bull, near the large testicles, where its scrotum is noticeably lighter in colour due to the frequent rubbing.

N. The National Museum of American Indian

One of three facilities, with the others being in Washington DC and Suitland/Maryland.

The George Gustav Heye Center, is based across two floors of the Alexander Hamilton U.S. Custom House and is named after the collector or native artefacts and objects over 54 years, beginning in 1903.

Heye was the son of a wealthy German immigrant, who had made his fortune in the petroleum industry. His own career in investment banking between 1901 and 1909 earned him

the wealth to fund his own archaeological expeditions and also those of scholars in the field.

Over the years, Heye managed to accumulate the largest private collection of Native American objects in the world - including both prehistoric and historic items. Initially he stored his collection in his Madison Avenue apartment, before moving it to a rented room.

O. Alexander Hamilton U.S. Custom House

Unusually facing away from the waterfront, which is not typical for Custom Houses, the exterior features an elaborate series of sculptures and motifs.

Twelve sculptures were hired to create the works from marble, with the most notable work consisting of the Four Continents on the front steps.

From east to west, the statues depict larger-than-life-size personifications of Asia, America, Europe, and Africa – with primary female figure in each group flanked by smaller human figures. In addition to the human depictions, Asia's figure is accompanied by a tiger, and Africa's figure is featuring a lion.

9. The White Horse

Located on one off the oldest blocks in New York, Bridge Street dates back to the original 17th century Dutch settlement. It is on the original the site of the Dutch West India Brewery.

When fur trader Philip Geraerdy become the first private tavern owner of the 'new world' in 1641 it was called The Wooden Horse Tavern, after a notable torture device of the era.

After changing the less controversially named White Horse the current building, dated to the mid-19th century, has housed cotton dealers, merchants and factories over the years.

Upon the repeal of prohibition, in 1933, the pub was reborn and has been under the ownership of the Gleeson family since 1976.

10. Fraunces Tavern

New Yorks oldest bar, established in 1762, is listed on the National Register of Historic Places.

Legend has it, that is once served as the watering hole for many of the Founding Fathers of the United States of America.

It achieved its fame as the site where, on December 4th 1783, nine days after the last British troops had left American soil, George Washington gathered a group of officers, to thank them for their service and bid an emotional farewell.

The Ghostbusters HQ, situated in the Firehouse of Hook & Ladder No. 8 (above) has worn the Ghostbusters logo since a fan donated it in 2022.

Opposite Mudville9, on Chambers Street, The Cary Building (above) was built in 1857 and is now largely used as a residential structure. As a result of the widening of Church Street in the 1920s, a 200-foot-long wall of unadorned brick is now exposed on the east side of the building.

The National September 11 Memorial & Museum (top) as seen from above features two square reflecting pools based around the footprints of the original World Trade Centre buildings that were destroyed in the 9/11 terrorist attacks. Ground Zero (above) required extensive rebuilding in the subsequent years with construction of the memorials commencing in 2006.

The roof detail of Alexander Hamilton U.S. Custom House (above) decorated throughout with nautical motifs such as dolphins and waves, interspersed with classical icons such as acanthus leaves and urns. It is unusual in that, unlike most custom houses (which face the waterfront), the Alexander Hamilton Custom House faces inland with its main entrance is on the northern façade. Nearby Battery Park (below) contains the 19th-centruy Castle Clinton, many ferry terminals and a 25-acre public space.

Hudson Yards to Chelsea Market

There is a fairly long walk in the middle of the route, but one worth making along the famous High Line.

Starting in the iconic Moynihan Train Station, the path leads through the glistening, newly developed, Hudson Yards, before a reasonable walk over (and through) the buildings into the Meatpacking District and the famous Chelsea Market.

It is best to avoid this route on Monday & Tuesday as a couple of the locations may be closed.

A particular highlight is Bathtub Gin, through its hidden door, although worth booking ahead as this opulent bar is often very busy.

Start from 34 Street, Penn Station (8th Avenue)

1. The Irish Exit   1:00pm
    421 8th Ave, NY 10001

2. Hudson Yards Tavern   1:30pm
    360 9th Ave, NY 10001

3. Maggie Reilly's   2:00pm
    340 9th Ave, NY 10001

4. Billymark's West   2:30pm
    332 9th Ave, NY 10001

5. The Bronx Brewery   3:15pm
    20 Hudson Yards Unit 207, NY 10001

6. The Standard Biergarten (closed Mon/Tues)   4:30pm
    848 Washington St, NY 10014

7. Brass Monkey   5:15pm
    55 Little W 12th St, NY 10014

8. Harlem Hops (closed Mon/Tues)   6:00pm
    at Pier 57, Market 57, 25 W 11th St, NY 10011

9. The Tippler   7:00pm
    425 W 15th St, NY 10011

10. Bathtub Gin   8:00pm
    132 9th Ave, NY 10011

11. The Canuck   9:00pm
    202 9th Ave, NY 10011

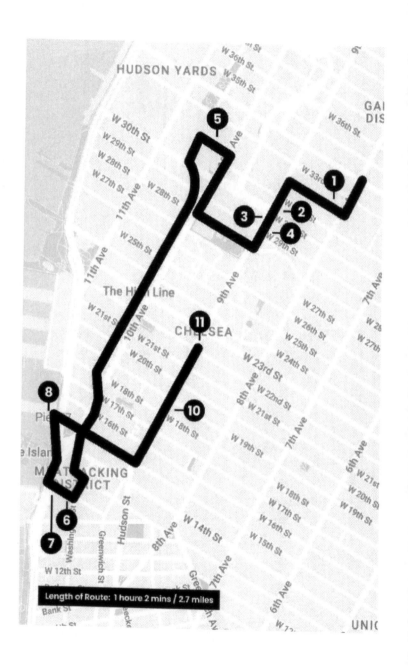

Length of Route: 1 hour 2 mins / 2.7 miles

Directions

Leave the station at 34th/8th and head into Moynihan Train Station **(A, B)** at one of the corners, opposite Madison Square Garden **(C)**, where **The Irish Exit (1)** is inside the first part of the station.

Continue through the station and turn left on 9th Avenue **(D)**, where **Hudson Yards Tavern (2)** is on the first block, with **Maggie Reilly's (3)** a few doors before **Billymark's West (4)** on the next block.

Cross to the next block, before crossing the road down West 28th Street past the park **(E)** and turning right onto 10th Avenue. Pass under The High Line, into Hudson Yards **F, G)** where **The Bronx Brewery (5)** is on the ground floor in the food hall.

Pass through the shopping centre **(H)**, following signs to Vessel **(I)** before turning left on The High Line **(J)**. After about 25 mins walk, exit onto West 14th Street and taking the first right, south, along Washington Street. Two blocks down, on Little West 12th Street, under The High Line is **The Standard Biergarten (6)** next to **Brass Monkey (7)**.

Past the pub, turn right at the main road, aiming to cross over as soon as possible to walk along The Empire State Trail **(K)** where Pier 57 **(L)** hosts **Harlem Hops (8)**.

Cross over the main road, heading down West 15th Street, and look out for the illuminated sign about halfway down the main block to **The Tippler (9)** underneath Chelsea Market **(M)**.

Continue past the pub, turning left onto 9th Avenue where **Bathtub Gin (10)** is hard to spot, as the hidden door is on the other side of the road, between W 18th & W 19th.

Much easier to find, is **The Canuck (11)** four blocks along on the same side of the road.

A. Moynihan Station

With a huge 21 tracks, the main commuter rail station of NYC is based in the city's former post office building and was built as an extension to Pennsylvania Station which, pre-Covid, saw 650,000 daily commuters.

It is named after US senator Daniel Moynihan, who originally commissioned the plans.

The total complex is 486,000 square feet and was built to alleviate congestion in nearby Penn Station. The renovation cost $1.6Bn and included a full restoration of the Beaux-Arts Farley building and the added construction of glass roof over a central atrium.

B. James Farley Post Office

Built between 1911-1914 thus Beaux-Arts style structure served as the main United States Postal Service branch before being repurposed as a train station.

The main facade of the Farley Building (on 8th Avenue) features a prominent Corinthian colonnade, which is the largest of its style in the world.

Above the colonnade, the entablature bears the inscription *"Neither snow nor rain nor heat nor gloom of night stays these couriers from the swift completion of their appointed rounds"*. This sentence is taken directly from Herodotus' Histories and describes the faithful service of the mounted Persian postal messengers under Xerxes I.

Whilst it is frequently mistaken as the official motto of the services is has become known as the United States Postal Service creed.

In summer 2020, Meta signed a lease for all 730,000 square feet of the office space in the Farley Building.

C. Madison Square Garden (MSG)

Opened in 1968, it is the fourth iteration with the first buildings being constructed in 1879 and 1890, located on East 26th Street.

It is the oldest arena in the NBA and NHL, as well hosting boxing, MMA, WWE, and many other sports events. It hosts more high-profile concerts than any other venue in NYC including from artists such as Michael Jackson, Elton John, Eric Clapton and U2.

Throughout the summer of 2017, Phish held 13 nights of concerts called *"The Bakers' Dozen", during* which they played 237 unique songs - repeating none during the entire run. A Phish themed banner was added to the rafters to commemorate the series of performances.

Billy Joel holds the record for the most appearances at the Garden with 134 shows.

1. The Irish Exit

Run by the award-winning founders of The Dead Rabbit – which claims to be the most awarded pub in the US.

Rumour has it that its name is a cheeky acknowledgement to the slang term *"Irish exit"* which is applied to anyone who leaves a party without saying goodbye Various studies appear to state that you can add up to two days of saved time to your life by foregoing those goodbyes.

D. Ninth Avenue

Originating just south of West 14th Street in the West Village, it extends uptown for 48 blocks until becoming Columbus Avenue (named after Christopher Columbus) at the intersection with West 59th Street.

A one-block stretch of Ninth Avenue between 15th and 16th Streets is also signed as *"Oreo Way"* as the first Oreo cookies were manufactured there at the former Nabisco headquarters, in 1912.

4. Billymark's West

Originally opened in 1956, since 1999, has been under the ownership of two brothers Mark and Billy Penza.

Over recent years, the brothers have cleaned up the iconic graffiti-tagged façade and covered the bathrooms with a fresh coat of paint, however the décor remains an eclectic mix with dozens of photos of The Beatles, framed gold and silver records, boxing gloves, posters of random '90s movies, a headshot of Elvis Costello and a Knicks clock, to name just a few.

E. Chelsea Park

This open public space that dates back to 1910, after being proposed in 1904 due to scarcity of public spaces along Ninth Avenue.

It is one of nine New York City parks with monuments to local heroes of WWI, with this featuring a statue to a WWI soldier, the *"Doughboy Statue"*, which was erected in 1921. Doughboy was a common a slang term for an infantryman.

The park also features two pairs of memorial gate posts, commissioned by the Horatio Seymour Tammany Club and installed in 1926 to commemorate the former borough president Frank L Dowling, the municipal civic court leader Frank J. Goodwin and the New York State Democratic Committee member William L. Kavanagh.

F. Hudson Yards (Development Area)

This huge redevelopment area is being completed in two phases with the first, opened in 2019, comprising of a public green space, eight residential structures that include hotels, offices and a shopping centre. The second phase aims to include further residential space, another office block and a school building.

It was initially intended for other developments, such as the West Side Stadium in the early 2000's, during the City's bid for the 2012 Summer Olympics.

Other possible constructions included new stadiums for both The Jets and The Yankees.

The current development has received mixed public approval with it being referred to as a *"gated community"* - alluding to the premium nature of the development, shops and residential offerings.

G. The Edge (30 Hudson Yards)

This skyscraper falls into the definition of 'Supertall' (which is over 150m but under 600m) and is the sixth-tallest in NYC and the eight-tallest in the US.

On its 100th floor is a unique open-air triangular observation deck, known as The Edge, which offers an intimidating view across NYC.

With a height of 1,100 feet, the deck is the world's second-highest outdoor observation platform that features transparent flooring.

H. Hudson Yards Shopping Centre

This high-end indoor shopping centre covers 1,000,000 sq. ft of retail and office space.

Upon opening, the shopping mall was anchored by Dior and Chanel, with a Fifth Avenue mix of shops such as H&M, Zara, and Sephora underneath them.

Following the Covid-19 pandemic many of the retail stores closed, including most of the restaurants, however there have been new establishments opening since.

I. Vessel (TKA)

Built to plans by the British designer Thomas Heatherwick, this visitor attraction is the iconic, main feature of the Hudson Yards Public Square.

It features an elaborate honeycomb-like structure that rises 16 stories and consists of 2,500 steps across 154 flights of stairs.

"Vessel" was planned to be the structure's temporary name during construction, with a permanent name to be determined later by popular vote. The TKA abbreviation in the structure's name stands for *"Temporarily Known As"*.

Whilst it has been referred to as *'Manhattan's answer to the Eiffel Tower'* by some it has also received criticism for its *'gaudy'* exterior. Although most objections tend to centre around the general malaise of the overall gated community and high-end nature of the developments as a whole.

J. The High Line

This redevelopment of the NYC Railroad spur is now a 1.45-mile-long linear park and walkway.

Inspired by the 1993 Coulée verte, in Paris, the park originates in the Meatpacking District before terminating at the newly developed Hudson Yards, near Javits Center.

After a decline in rail traffic, the track was abandoned in 1980 when the construction of the Javits Center required the demolition of the viaduct's northernmost section.

Since opening in the summer of 2009, the park has grown to over eight million visitors each year with tourists accounting for 4/5 of all visits.

It is maintained by Friends of the High Line, which was founded by Joshua David and Robert Hammond, and the organization is credited with saving the structure and convincing Mayor Michael Bloomberg's administration in 2002 to support the regeneration project. The organisation is responsible for a budget of around $5m a year.

6. The Standard Biergarten

The 200-seater venue, is based under the steel beams of The High Line and provides both the grittiness of the NYC Meatpacking district with the lovely atmosphere you would expect in German Beer Hall.

K. Little Island

This artificial island at Pier 55 covers 2.4 acres and is created out of 132 pot-shaped structures that referred to as 'Tulips'.

The 'tulip pots' vary in height and are between 15-62 ft above the waterline. The style and heights of the pots were intended to give the appearance of a floating leaf.

With a capacity of 1,000 visitors, the island features a small stage and a 687-seat amphitheatre that hosts mainly free events. By 2023 over 570 shows had been presented to over 3 million visitors.

L. Pier 57

Having undergone extensive renovations in the early 2010s, it is currently operated by Google and serves as a campus for employees, before opening to the public.

It replaced the original wooden pier, built in 1907, that was largely destroyed in a large fire during the autumn of 1947. Construction began in 1950 and at the time it was the largest dock building effort ever undertaken by the City of New York.

8. Harlem Hops

Manhattan's first 100% African-American owned craft beer bar, based inside Pier 57, offers a large range of small-batch, local beers. This is their satellite branch with the main location and brewery in Harlem.

9. The Tippler

Nestled in the cellar space, underneath Chelsea Market, the entrance to the bar is spotted under the illuminated sign along West 15th Street.

M. Chelsea Market

Occupying the entire block between Ninth and Tenth Avenues, this large food hall and retail space was constructed in 1890's on the site of the National Biscuit Company's Factory (known as Nabisco) – where the Oreo was invented and produced.

It was redeveloped to its current use in the 1990's and is owned by Google's Parent Company – Alphabet.

10. Bathtub Gin

First appearing in 1920, in the prohibition-era United States, this term references to the poor-quality alcohol that was common at the time.

With gin being the predominant drink during the 1920's, many variations were created in vessels large enough to supply commercial users but small enough for the operation to go undetected by the police.

This made the mixing of cheap grain alcohol with water and flavourings and other agents, such as juniper berry juice and glycerine in a common metal bathtub ideal.

However, as distillation requires boiling and condensation in a closed apparatus, it cannot be accomplished in an open vessel, meaning stories of 'bathtub' gin are more likely to be urban legend than fact.

11. The Canuck

The origins for this slang term for a Canadian are unknown, however it is commonly used as an affectionate term. Originally recorded at 'Kanuck' in 1835, by the 1850's it had switched to the spelling with a 'c'.

The glass covered atrium of Moynihan Train Sation overlooking its neighbour, the famous Madison Square Garden with The Empire State Building in the background.

The 486,000 sq. ft complex was designed by Skidmore, Owings & Merrill, and houses 31,000 sq. ft passenger concourse underneath an iconic 92ft tall glass skylight.

119

Opened in 2019, the culture centre at The Shed (above) commissions, produces, and presents a wide range of activities in performing arts, visual arts, and pop culture in its 500-seat theatre; and across two levels of exhibition space. The Javits Centre (below) was completed in 1986 and, with over 3.3m sq. ft is billed as one of the busiest convention centres in the world.

Vessel (top) has been referred to as 'The Giant Shawarma' by commentators due to its unusual shape. The High Line observation deck (bottom) on Tenth Avenue Square provides views of the city, following the removal of several steel beams.

Train passing through the Bell Laboratories Building, on The High Line (above) seen from Washington Street in 1936. In 2018 Alphabet purchased Chelsea Market (below) for more than $2.4Bn, which was described as the most expensive real estate transaction in NYC history.

Hell's Kitchen to The Rock

This walk leads from the North of Hell's Kitchen, past some of the city's oldest buildings on the banks of the Hudson River. It features the famous Landmark Tavern, before heading East through one of the world's busiest tourist hotspots at Times Square before ending up at The Rockefeller Centre.

It is a great route to absorb the stark differences between the notoriously gritty Hell's Kitchen and the glitz and commercialism of the billboards of Times Square.

Concluding at one of the most iconic city locations, The Rockefeller Centre, at the edge of the famous shopping destination of 5th Avenue.

The iconic Landmark Tavern is a particular highlight, with its old building standing proud amongst the developments.

Start from 59 St-Columbus Circle Metro

1. All Stars Sports Bar & Grill   2:00pm
   327 W 57th St, NY 10019

2. D.J. Reynolds   2:30pm
   351 W 57th St, NY 10019

3. Valhalla NYC   3:00pm
   815 9th Ave, NY 10019

4. Alfie's Craft Beer Bar   3:30pm
   800 9th Ave, NY 10019

5. The Waylon   4:15pm
   736 10th Ave, NY 10019

6. The Landmark Tavern   5:00pm
   626 11th Ave, NY 10036

7. Hellcat Annie's Tap Room   6:00pm
   637 10th Ave, NY 10036

   Scruffy Duffy's
   639 10th Ave, NY 10036

8. The Brazen Tavern   7:00pm
   356 W 44th St, NY 10036

9. The Playwright   8:00pm
   202 W 49th St, NY 10019

10. Pig 'N' Whistle   9:00pm
    58 W 48th St, NY 10036

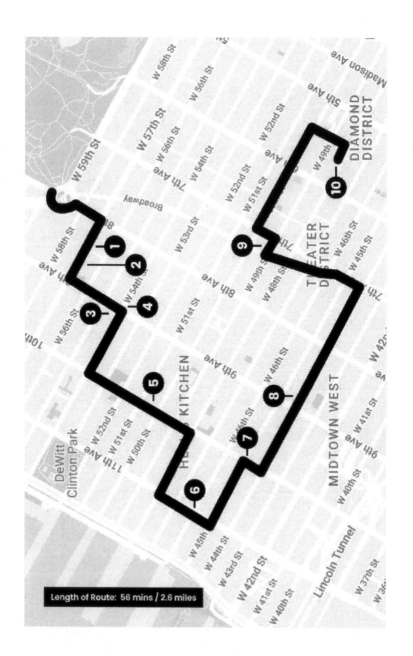

Length of Route: 56 mins / 2.6 miles

Directions

Head over the roundabout **(A, B)**, down 8th Avenue, away from the park and take the 2nd right on West 57th Street. **All Stars Sports Bar & Grill (1)** in next to **D. J. Reynolds (2)**.

Continue past the pub and take the first left onto 9th Avenue. After 3 blocks, **Valhalla NYC (3)** is on the corner of 54th & 9th with **Alfie's Craft Beer Bar (4)** opposite.

Cross the road, towards the Hudson, down West 52nd Street, and turn left at 10th Avenue **(C)** where **The Waylon (5)** is on this block.

Continue down 10th Avenue **(D)**, before crossing and heading down West 48th Street where **The Landmark Tavern (6)** is on the corner of 11th Avenue a couple of blocks down.

Turn left out of the pub down 11th Avenue, before turning first left onto West 45th Street. At the end of the block there is a choice between **Hellcat Annies (7)** or **Scruffy Duffy's**.

Continue down West 45th Street before turning right on 9th Avenue, where **The Brazen Tavern (8)** is just down West 44th Street. Follow this road all the way to 7th Avenue, where a left turn leads to Times Square **(E, F)**. Brave the crowds by passing by the famous red steps **(G)** to the left. **The Celtic Pub/Playwright (9)** is right, down West 49th Street.

Head along 7th Avenue, and turn right down West 50th Street. Continue past Radio City **(H)** and take a right through The Rockefeller Centre's **(I)** pedestrian zone, over two blocks **(J)**, before turning right at West 48th Street where **Pig 'N' Whistle (10)** is across the road.

A. Columbus Circle

Whilst roundabouts are generally quite unusual in the US, this buys intersection is the central point from which all distances from New York City are measured.

It is named after the Italian explorer whose Spanish originated voyages across the Atlantic paved the way for European colonisation and expansion of the Americas.

The 76ft central monument towers over the traffic and was erected in 1892.

It became comparable to Speakers Corner, in London, as a location for soapbox orators in the mid-20th-century. In contrast to the more liberal location of Union Square, it became host to a number of far-right speakers, cranks and street preachers.

It is the location of the manifestation of the Stay Puff Marshmallow man in 1984 hit comedy Ghostbusters.

B. Billionaires Row

Notable for a number of supertall, pencil towers on 57th Street, the surrounding area is known to contain some of the most expensive residences in the world.

Michael Dell purchased the top two floors of One57 for $100m in 2015. It set the record for the most expensive apartment ever sold in New York, before the $238m purchase, by hedge fund manager Kenneth Griffin, of the top 4 floors of 220 Central Park South.

Although most properties have been purchased through shell companies or trust funds, at least 17 owners have been identified as billionaires, including the likes of Daniel Loeb, Jerry Yang, Pan Shiyi, Eyal Ofer and Sara Blakely.

The 435m high Steinway Tower holds the world record as the thinnest skyscraper in the world, is 24 times taller than it is wide and only has one residence per floor.

3. Valhalla NYC

This majestic hall, located in Asgard, is present in Norse mythology as the destination for half of those who die in combat – the other half reside with Freyja in Folkvangr.

C. Hell's Kitchen

Historically the bastion of the poor and working-class Irish immigrants, Hell's Kitchen's gritty reputation and poor transport links has typically kept its real estate prices lower than other parts of Manhattan.

It is not certain where the name originally came from and there are several explanations.

Early uses appear in comments from Davy Crockett; other mentions link a German restaurant 'Heils Kitchen' as a possible source of the name.

Whilst most fire stations lost firefighters in the 9/11 terrorist attacks, the team at 48th Street, who specialised in skyscraper fires, lost 15 members.

The area is also home to the USS Intrepid Sea, Air and Space Museum, which is stationed at Peir 86 on the Hudson River, which is based around the WWII Aircraft carrier of the same name.

5. The Waylon

This country music bar is home to a wooden mascot called 'Haggard' and serves a signature 'Hail Bloody Mary' to the Green Bay Packers Fan Club.

D. Hell's Kitchen Park

With residents complaining about the limited open space in the 1960's, the New York state government acquired and developed this land for about $400,000 in 1966 – however it was not until 1979 when the playground eventually opened to the public.

6. The Landmark Tavern

When Patrick Henry Carley opened this Irish Saloon, in 1868, it would have sat on the shores of the, pre-Twelfth Avenue, banks of the Hudson River.

During prohibition the living space on the 2nd and 3rd floors were converted into a speakeasy.

A favourite haunt of the notoriously violent Irish gang 'The Westies' in the 1980's legend has it that three ghosts haunt this old tavern.

The first ghost is the spirit of George Raft, the Hollywood bruiser who grew up nearby; the second is that of a Confederate Civil War veteran who, after begin stabbed, died in a bathtub that remains on the second floor; finally, the third ghost is that of a young Irish girl who was said to have died of cholera after immigrating to escape the potato famine.

7. Hellcat Annies (or Scruffy Duffy's)

Once the headquarters of the infamous 'Westies' who were a violent gang with ties to the mafia.

Although typically between 12-20 members at any time, they are rumoured to have accounted for 60-100 murders between 1968 and 1986.

Formed in the early 1960's when the 'Gentleman Gangster', as he became to be known, Mickey Spillane moved in to the area due to an exodus of gang leaders trying to avoid prosecution.

Serving as an apprentice to Hughie Mulligan, he cemented his power through marriage to the daughter of the prestigious McManus family.

The gang was responsible for racketeering and contract killing. Amongst their other activities were bookmaking, loansharking, and the unpleasant activity of snatching local business and holding them to ransom.

Spillane was assassinated by Gambino family hitman, Roy DeMeo, as part of the Irish-Italian mob war, outside his Queens apartment in 1977.

E. One Times Square

Although barely visible behind the billboards and signage, this iconic building hosts some of the most valuable advertiser real estate on the planet.

Construction completed in 1904, it is most recognised for the New Years Eve 'Ball Drop' which first occurred in 1907.

Originally the offices for *The New York Times* – which gives the square its name – it has passed across several owners during its lifetime, before Lehmen Brothers acquired it in 1995 and started adding billboards to take advantage of its location.

One of the most notable early billboards was a large Cup Noodles design, that featured rising steam from behind the advertisement.

F. Nasdaq Market Site

This 8-story LED screen, that occupies the base of 4 Time Square is the commercial marketing presence of the Nasdaq Stock Market which is, along with the New York Stock Exchange, one of the most active exchanges in the world.

Opened on 1st January 2000, the display was the largest in the world at the time of its completion.

G. Father Duffy Square

Whilst the northern triangle of Times Square is most recognised for the red steps, in front of them is a statue of Francis Duffy who became the most highly decorated cleric in the history of the US army.

As chaplain for the 69th Infantry Regiment, he was known to follow soldiers into the heart of the conflict to tend to the wounded or recover injured soldiers.

The statue was erected, and the square dedicated to Duffy, by March 1939, with the street signs changed by June.

H. Radio City

Opened as part of the Rockefeller Center in December 1932, it nicknamed *'The Showplace of the Nation'*, it is the headquarters for precision dance company the Rockettes.

When it opened, the 5,960-seater, four-tier auditorium was the largest in the world.

Although intended to host stage productions, it was quickly converted into a movie theatre within a year of opening and was the site of several movie premieres – with the first feature film being Frank Capra's 'The Bitter Tea of General Yen.'

Towards the late 1970's attendances had declined to an all-time low of less than 1.5m – significantly under the 4m annual visitors it needed to break even.

The management, at the time, began exploring alternative uses to convert the theatre such as tennis courts, hotel accommodation, retail space, a theme park, and aquarium or the American Stock Exchange.

After a public campaign, development plans were stifled as the premises was granted landmark status in 1985. Music concerts became more common and the venue started to make its first profits for over 30 years.

Its popularity increased as it started hosting live televised events and awards ceremonies such as The Grammys, Tonys, MTV Video Music Awards and the NFL draft.

I. Rockefeller Center

Covering 22 acres of Midtown Manhattan, the Rockefeller Center, commissioned by the family of the same name, contains 19 commercial buildings, with the original 14 built in the Art Deco style and span the area between Fifth and Sixth Avenues.

To begin construction a staggering 228 buildings were demolished and over 4,000 residents relocated. Whilst almost every lease had been purchased by 1931, a couple of holdout buildings refused to sell and abut the north and south corners of the 30 Rockefeller Plaza annex.

J. NBC Studios

Located in the Rockefeller Plaza, the building hoses the network headquarters and its flagship station, WNBC.

The current studio space is occupied by some of the most famous US shows such as Saturday Night Live, The Tonight Show Starring Jimmy Fallon and the Kelly Clarkson Show.

10. Pig 'N' Whistle

In the West Midlands, England, workers in the iron foundry would need to keep hydrated, working in such extreme heat, so would attach leather tankards, known colloquially as Piggens, to their belts.

Although ale was not allowed, they would summon a water boy, with a large jug of water, by blowing a whistle incorporated into the handle.

Over time these tankards became known as Piggen Whistles, which resulted in the pub name Pig & Whistle.

Landmark Tavern (above) is one of the oldest drinking haunts in Manhattan, having been established in 1868. Located on at Pier 86 on the Hudson River, the USS Intrepid, alongside the concord (below) is the major exhibit in the Sea, Air and Space Museum.

The New Years Eve 'Ball Drop' (above) attracts over 100,000 to the square. The 'tkts' concession booth (below) was first opened in 1973 and has become a landmark .

The impressive auditorium of Radio City Music Hall (top) was the largest in the world at its time of opening – as well as hosting the world's largest orchestra, the most expansive theatre screen and the heaviest proscenium arch. With the lights on, the famous exterior (below) is one of the most recognisable sights of the Rockefeller Center,

Lunch atop a Skyscraper is a black-and-white photograph of eleven ironworkers sitting on a steel beam at the 69th floor of the RAC Building. Taken in 1932, the photo, 850 feet above the ground, was arranged as a publicity stunt as part of a campaign promoting the skyscraper. The Rockefeller Plaza is key location for festive activities (below) in New York City with an estimated 125 million visitors each year.

Lincoln Square to Upper West Side

This short route, explores the Irish pubs and dive bars tucked behind the impressive American Museum of Natural History.

Passing the spot where John Lennon was tragically murdered, the path follows the edge of the famous park, before heading back, adjacent to Broadway, and the busy thoroughfare of Amsterdam Avenue.

This route is perfect for a reasonably short walk, with great spots along the way to stop and eat.

The city's only all-female-owned Sports bar, Blondies, is well worth a special visit, as is Dead Poets and George Keeley at the end of the route.

Start from 72nd Street Metro

1. Emerald Inn   1:30pm
    250 W 72nd Street, NY 10023

2. Malachy's   2:15pm
    103 W 72nd Street, NY 10023

3. Dive 75   4:00pm
    101 W 75th Street, NY 10023

4. Amsterdam Ale House   4:45pm
    340 Amsterdam Avenue, NY 10024

5. Blondies Sports   5:30pm
    225 W 79th Street, NY 10024

6. Dublin House   6:00pm
    225 W 79th Street, NY 10024

7. The Dead Poet   6:45pm
    450 Amsterdam Avenue #2, NY 10024

8. Fred's   7:15pm
    476 Amsterdam Avenue, NY 10024

9. Hi Life Bar & Grill   7:45pm
    477 Amsterdam Avenue, NY 10024

10. George Keeley   8:30pm
    485 Amsterdam Avenue, NY 10024

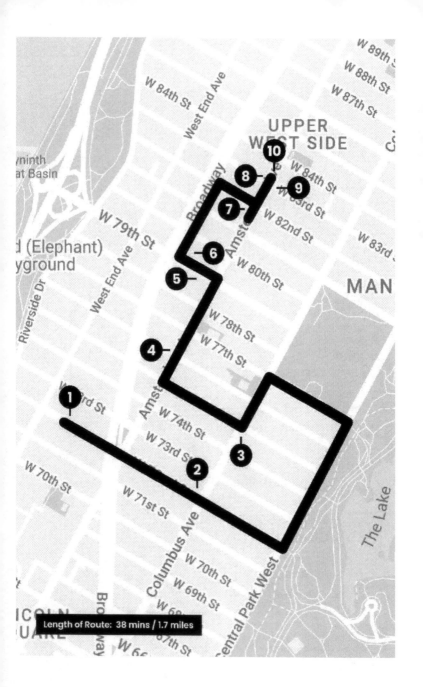

Length of Route: 38 mins / 1.7 miles

Directions

Exit the and head away from the park, with Verdi Square **(A)** on the other side of the road, where **Emerald Inn (1)** is on the left. Turn back and walk past the station, over Broadway where **Malachy's (2)** is on the corner of 72nd/Columbus.

Whilst the next pub is only two blocks left, it is more scenic to walk towards the park, turning left at the Dakota **(B, C)**, along Central Park West **(D, E)**, before turning left onto West 77th Street past the museum **(F)**. Head back down Columbus Avenue where **Dive 75 (3)** is on the right, just down West 75th Street.

Continue past the pub, turning right at Beacon Theatre **(G)** on the next junction where **Amsterdam Ale House (4)** is on the corner of the next block.

Exit the pub left, heading up Amsterdam Avenue, before turning left onto West 70th Street where **Blondies (5)** is on the left, with **Dublin House (6)** opposite.

Continue past the pub and turn right at Broadway, before turning right onto West 82nd Street after a couple of blocks. **The Dead Poet (7)** is to the right on Amsterdam Avenue.

Exit the pub left and continue a couple of blocks before reaching **Fred's (8)** on the corner, opposite **Hi Life Bar & Grill (9)** with **George Keeley (10)** just a couple of doors further down Amsterdam Avenue.

A. Verdi Square

Named after the Italian Opera composer and featuring the Giuseppe Verdi monument, which was constructed in 1906.

The huge monument is 25-feet tall and 18-feet across, with the dark granite pedestal featuring statues of four main characters from Verdi's operas: Aida, Otello, Leonora of La forza del destino, and Falstaff.

B. The Dakota

Constructed in the Germain Renaissance style and completed in 1884, it was one of the first large developments in the Upper West Side and the oldest luxury apartments in the city.

Although notable residents include the likes of Judy Garland, Roberta Flack, Boris Karloff, Connie Chung, Paul Simon and Joe Namath it is also notable for the famous faces that have been refused residence by the boards notoriously high standards of approval.

Names refused include Billy Joel, Madonna, Gene Simmons, Cher and Judd Apatow.

For all its cultural impact, architecture and famous residents it is most notable as the site of John Lennon's murder in 1980.

C. The Murder of John Lennon

The legendary former Beatle, was shot and killed on the steps of The Dakota on the evening of 8th December 1980, by a jealous fan who had become enraged by Lennon's rich lifestyle and claims that The Beatles were more popular than Jesus.

Obsessed with J.D. Salinger's novel, Catcher in the Rye, the killer spent several months planning and had met Lennon earlier that evening to have his copy of 'Double Fantasy' signed, before returning a few hours later and firing five hollow-point bullets, four of which hit Lennon in the back.

After Lennon was pronounced dead his wife, Yoko Ono, who was present at the murder, asked the Roosevelt Hospital not to report her husbands passing to the media until she had informed their five-year-old son Sean, who was still in the Hotel.

The public response was huge, with millions around the world pausing for 10mins silence, a few days later, on 14th December.

His last album, Double Fantasy, which was released three weeks beforehand, initially receiving a mixed critical reaction and low sales, became a worldwide success and won the 1981 Grammy Award for Album of the Year.

An area of Central Park, opposite The Dakota, was landscaped renamed Strawberry Fields, after The Beatles Song, with a mosaic featuring the title of Lennon's most famous song 'Imagine.'

D. Central Park

Chosen as the site of a managed public park, ahead of Jones Wood, this 843-acre green space is the most visit US urban park, attracting over 40m visitors each year.

Planning officially began in 1840's as the city's population quadrupled between 1820's to 1855, and the main open spaces, and escape from urban life, were cemeteries.

Initially the 160-acre wooded area on Upper East Site called Jones Wood was chosen, however this met strong opposition due to its unfavourable location and unreasonable bill to acquire the land.

Central Park offered a more central city location, and the 150m gallon collecting reservoir was well positioned as the geographical centre.

In 1853 the New York State Legislature passed the Central Park Act, which authorised the purchase of what is now the present-day site of Central Park.

The final design for the park was selected in 1858 with the designers, Frederick Law Olmsted and Calvert Vaux, taking inspiration from Birkenhead Park on the Wirral, in England, which is widely regarded as the first publicly funded park in the world.

The park is surrounded by a stone wall which is 8,847m long and 1.1m high, with 18, initially unnamed, gates.

In more recent times, Central Park is one of the most filmed locations in the world and over 231 movies have been filmed on location – compared to 160 in Greenwich Village and 99 in Times Square.

Famous films include Hitch, Home Alone 2, Maid in Manhattan, 13 going on 30, The Fisher King and Enchanted.

E. The Concert in Central Park

With the state of the park deteriorating in the 1970's and the city struggling to raise the estimated $3m required to return it to its former glory, a non-profit was founded in 1980 to begin a campaign to raise funds.

The idea of a free open-air concert was developed from the past successes of Elton John and James Taylor, with Simon & Garfunkel approached as the ideal choice to headline.

Their New York roots, coupled with their recent popularity, meant they were likely to draw a large crowd.

Taking place on the Great Lawn on 19th September 1981, the organisers anticipated 300,000 attendees but, although rain had fallen continuously throughout the day, over 500,000 revellers made this one of the largest concerts in US history.

Their set list of 21 songs featured all their major hits, from Mrs. Robinson to Bridge over Troubled Water, before ending with The Sound of Silence.

The concert was received favourably by music critics, with the accompanying album selling over 2m copies.

F. American Museum of Natural History

Constructed in 1877, this vast museum occupies 2.5m sq. ft and holds approximately 35 million different specimens of plants, fungi, animals, fossils, rocks, minerals and cultural artifacts.

As it has expanded over the years, the building has grown to consist of twenty buildings that house a total of 45 permanent exhibition halls, such as 'Mammals Hall', 'Human Origins & Cultural Halls', 'Earth and Planetary Science Halls' and 'Fossil Halls'.

The first Dinosaur Hall opened in 1905 and features a Tyrannosaurus competed almost entirely from real fossil bones – combined from two specimens that were discovered in the US.

Although mostly shot on a sound stage in Vancouver, the book and subsequent film 'Night at the Museum' is set here, with the museums faced being used for the exterior shots.

3. Dive 75

Although the precise definition of a 'dive bar' is rarely agreed on, they are typically small, unglamorous drinking establishments that feature dim lighting, dated décor and inexpensive drinks.

The term dive first came to prominence in the US press during the 1880's to describe the disreputable places that were often in basements or hidden in the 'dives below'.

G. Beacon Theatre

Despite its relatively plain exterior, this 2,894-seat theatre was opened in 1929 and features an interior that is listed as a NYC Interior Landmark and spans styles, including Renaissance, Ancient Roman, Ancient Greek, and Rococo-inspired elements

The Beacon is one of only three theatres in Manhattan that retains its original Wurlitzer organ - Radio City Music Hall and the United Palace are the others.

Despite the organ no longer working, by the early 1960s, it was not removed because the cost was too high at the time.

4. Amsterdam Ale House

There has been a bar since prohibition ended in the 1930's, first as Sweeney's, then J.G. Melon's in the 1980's, West Side Brewing Company from 1993-2000's before finally becoming Amsterdam Ale House.

Originally founded by the Dutch, in the 17th-century, the settlement at Manhattan was first know as New Amsterdam before the English took control and renamed it after the King's brother, The Duke of York.

6. Dublin House

Opened during the prohibition era in the 1920's, it began operating officially in 1933 with the neon harp acting as a nearby beacon and often the first thing that docking sailors, from the 79th Street Boat Basin saw.

The Neon sign was restored through a crowdfunding campaign to bring it to its former glory.

7. Dead Poets

The bar owner was once an English teacher and he, as a nod to his academic past, has hung framed verses from Dickinson, Donne, and Joyce on the walls.

1989 coming-of-age drama, Dead Poets Society, tells the tale of an English Teacher (played by Robin Williams) who inspires his students with poetry.

In the film, the boys form 'The Dead Poets Society' where they privately read poetry together. When one of the boys commits suicide, the group are pressured into letting their teacher take the fall.

8. Fred's

Named after a female black Labrador who was bred by the Guiding Eyes for the Blind, whose dogs play important roles as guides and companions for the visually impaired.

Whilst each litter is put through a stringent training programme, not every dog has the required aptitude meaning that there is large waiting list to rehome the puppies that miss out.

Fred was adopted by the bars owners, and the walls are adorned with images of 'man's best friend'.

9. Hi Life Bar & Grill

Set with 1930's décor, the vintage neon sign compliments the art deco bar, cozy booths and banquette seating.

10. George Keeley

The current owners also used to own Dead Poets and the two bars share a theme, by recording either the pints of Guinness drunk or different beers tried by their patrons with the most guzzling being rewarding with their names on plaques adorning the walls.

If you manage to sample 100 different beers, then you are rewarded with a lifetime discount of 20% off.

Located at the southeast corner of Riverside Park, the Eleanor Roosevelt Monument (above) is the first work of public art in NYC to be dedicated to an American woman. During her husband's time in office her travels, public engagement, and advocacy, largely redefined the role of First Lady. The Verdi Monument (over) imposing construction, towers over the small public space overlooking 72nd Street Station.

The vast central atrium (above) of the Richerd Gilder Centre for Education is an impressive addition to the American Museum of Natural History. The Milstein Hall of Ocean Life (below), contains a 94ft model of a Blue Whale suspended from the ceiling.

The impressive interior of the Beacon Theatre (above) is listed on the national register of historic places. Opened in 1929, it has hosted film screenings before returning to live shows after a failed conversion into a nightclub. The Allman Brothers Band was, at one point, the most frequent resident performer, opening its 40th anniversary event (below) at the Beacon.

Union Square to Alphabet City

This direct walk explores the unusual bars and pubs in the eclectic areas around East Village before ending at the unusually named Alphabet City.

The route features some of the city's oldest pubs including the famous Pete's Tavern, McSorley's and the picturesque Old Town Bar.

It is a simple route to follow, and explore the area, before ending at Royale's which claims to have been voted the best burger in NYC.

Start from 23rd Street Subway Station

1. Old Town Bar   1:00pm
   45 E 18th Street, NY 10003

2. Pete's Tavern   1:45pm
   129 E 18th Street, NY 10003

3. The Penny Farthing   2:30pm
   103 3rd Avenue, NY 10003

4. McSorley's Old Ale House   3:15pm
   15 E 7th Street, NY 10003

5. The Scratcher   4:00pm
   209 E 5th Street, NY 10003

6. Tom & Jerry's   4:45pm
   288 Elizabeth Street, NY 10012

7. Fool's Gold   5:30pm
   145 E Houston Street, NY 10002

8. d.b.a.   6:15pm
   41 1st Avenue, NY 10003

9. Doc Holliday's   7:15pm
   141 Avenue A, NY 10009

10. Royale   8:00pm
    157 Loisaida Ave, NY 10009

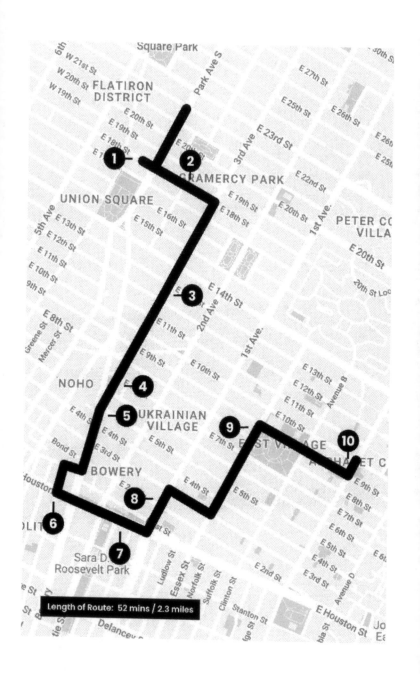

Directions

Head south on Park Avenue and turn right after a few blocks, down East 18th Street, where **Old Town Bar (1)** is in the middle of the block. Turn left out of the pub, back over Park Avenue South, and **Pete's Tavern (2, A)** is on the corner of the next block.

Continue past the pub on East 18th Street, and turn right at 3rd Avenue and pass a few blocks to **The Penny Farthing (3, B)** on the corner of 13th/3rd. Continue down 3rd Avenue, several blocks, until taking a left **(C)** onto East 7th Street where **McSorley's Old Ale House (4)** is a few doors down.

Head back to 3rd Avenue and continue a couple of blocks before turning left onto East 5th Street where **The Scratcher (5)** is hidden in the basement of 209.

Head back to 3rd Avenue and turn left along the main road, after several blocks cross over and head down Bleeker Street, before taking the first left along Elizabeth Street where **Tom and Jerry's (6)** is at the end of the block. Turn left at the main road, and **Fools Gold (7)** is across the road, on the block after Houston Street Playground.

Continue past the pub, and turn left at the first junction, to find **d.b.a (8)** on the left in the second block.

Cross the road and head down East 3rd Street, before turning left at the end of the block along Avenue A, where **Doc Holliday's (9)** is on the left, a few blocks up, opposite the park.

Leave the pub and head directly over the Tompkins Square Park **(D)**, past Charlie Parker's Residence **(E)** onto East 9th Street, turning left at the end of the block onto Avenue C where **Royale (10)** is on the corner **(F)**.

1. Old Town Bar

Open since 1892, it was originally a German tavern called Viemeisters but during prohibition it changed to Craig's Restaurant and started serving food in order to operate as a speakeasy.

Many of the original fixtures, dating back to the 19th-century, remain with the 55ft bar made of mahogany and marble. The high ceiling features pressed steel tiles.

It has retained the original wooden staircase, antique cash registers, wooden booths and old mirrors.

As well as notable, old-style urinals in the first-floor gents' toilets, it has New York's oldest dumbwaiter to ferry food between the kitchen and bar.

The pub is notable for its appearances in several films, television shows and music videos including House of Pain's 'Jump around,' Sex and the City and in the opening montage of Late Night with David Letterman.

2. Pete's Tavern

Constructed in 1851 as the Portman Hotel, the downstairs was used as a drinking establishment from 1864.

The 40-ft rosewood bar, decorated back bar, tin ceiling and tile flooring are all original fixtures, dating back to its opening and the booths and cabinets have been used since it became a restaurant – known as 'Healy's Café' in 1899.

Peter D'Belles purchase the café in 1922 and renamed it 'Pete's Tavern'.

During Prohibition, the bar was disguised as a florist, with the exterior adorned with fresh flowers. Whilst signs outside invited patrons in through the side door, in what is now the first dining room, before providing the password and then sneaking through a dummy refrigerator door.

A. Gift of the Magi

Written in the booth of Pete's Tavern, this short tells of a young husband and wife dealing with the challenge of buying secret Christmas gifts for each other with very little money.

First published in 1905, the sentimental story remains popular for its simple plot and twist at the end.

B. Emma Goldman Plaque

A few doors down E 13th Street, from The Penny Farthing, is this plaque dedicated to the anarchist revolutionary Emma Goldman.

Born in Lithuania, she played a pivotal role in the development of anarchist political philosophy in North America before being deported to the Russian Empire in 1940.

3. The Penny Farthing

This early type of bicycle was popular in the 1870's and 1880's and, because of its distinctive large front wheel, was also known as a high wheel or high wheeler.

The large wheel enabled the rider to cover a large distance at high speed and a more comfortable journey with its shock absorption qualities.

The name, although likely not widely used until they were replaced by more modern bikes, came from the British penny and farthing coins - the penny being much larger than the farthing, resembled the side angle of the bicycle.

They became obsolete towards the end of the 1880's as the invention of chain-driven modern bikes, with pneumatic tyres, offered greater safety and speed.

C. The Cooper Union Speech

Delivered by Abraham Lincoln on 27th February 1860, at the Cooper Union Building, it is considered one of the most important speeches leading to his victory in the US Presidential Elections.

His speech, which was well-researched and contained over 7,000 words, was hurriedly re-written the night before when he learnt that the venue had been moved from the Henry Ward Beechers Church.

The speech was a masterful political move. Delivered in the home state of the favoured candidate for the 1860 election, William H. Seward, and attended by Presidential-kingmaker Horace Greeley, the speech positioned Lincoln to challenge for the Presidential nomination.

4. McSorley's Old Ale House

Generally known simply as McSorley's, it is believed to be the oldest Irish saloon in New York City, having opened in the mid-19th century.

It is considered to be one of the longest continuously operating ale houses in the city mainly due to the fact that during Prohibition it served a *"near beer"* with too little alcohol to be illegal and ensured it was able to remain trading.

With aged artwork, newspapers covering the wall and spit and sawdust floors, McSorley's has an atmosphere reminiscent of *"Olde New York"*. Legend has it that no piece of memorabilia has been removed from the walls since 1910, alongside many items of historical significance, such as a pair of Harry Houdini's handcuffs, which are connected to the bar rail.

When the New York Rangers hockey team won the Stanley Cup. in 1994, they took the trophy to McSorley's and drank out of it, creating a dent that needed several days to repair.

5. The Scratcher

Irish slang for 'bed,' being 'on the scratch' is also a term for unemployment. This basement bar is hard to spot

6. Tom and Jerry's

Taking its name from the vast collection of pottery and glassware displayed behind the bar – a huge selection of cups, pots and bowls inscribed with the name of the infamous cat-and-mouse duo.

The eponymous duo featured in 161 short films, for Metro-Goldwyn-Mayer, after their 1940 creation by Willaim Hanna and Joseph Barbera.

Initially producing 114 shorts between 1940 to 1958, the Hanna-Barbera combo won 7 Oscars for best Animated Short Film.

Although largely looked back on favourably, like many animated cartoons between the 1930's to 1950's, Tom and Jerry often featured racial stereotypes.

The most controversial character in the show is Mammy Two Shoes, who is depicted as a poor black maid who speaks with a strong accent.

During the 1960's versions of the shorts replaced the African-American maid with a white woman with an Irish accent, voiced by June Foray.

In modern times, In The Simpsons, The Itchy & Scratchy Show is a spoof of Tom and Jerry.

7. Fool's Gold

The nickname for the mineral pyrite which is the most abundant sulphide mineral, with its brass-yellow hue give it a superficial resemblance to gold.

It is also the title of the 1989 hit, by iconic British rock band The Stone Roses. Their first single to reach the UK Top-10 charts, it was by far their biggest commercial hit at the time.

NME magazine placed the song at number 31 in their "500 Greatest Songs of All Time" list in 2014.

8. d.b.a.

There is a long-running debate as to whether the acronym stands for "doing business as," "don't bother asking," or "drink better ale." This is one of the dog-friendly bars that allows dogs inside, although it also has a large patio area that resembles a German Beer Garden at the back.

9. Doc Holliday's

Opened in 1994, this bar carries the style and vibe of an old school honky tonk. Its jukebox holds a huge collection of country music.

D. Tomkins Square Park

Covering 10.5 acres, this public space opening in 1834 and is named after Daniel D. Tompkins – the Vice-President of the USA from 1817 to 1825.

The square has been the location of many mass demonstrations and activism.

In 1857, immigrants protesting unemployment and food shortages were attacked by police, before the deadly Draft Riots occurred later, in 1863, in the park.

The change to a more modern layout of the park in 1936 was rumoured to be intended to divide and manage protesting crowds. A tradition that was rekindled as the park became the home of demonstrations against the Vietnam War in the 1960s.

By the 1980s the park had become for synonymous with the city's increased social problems and was an area of high crime, encampments of homeless people, and a centre for illegal drug dealing and heroin use.

E. Charlie Parker Residence

A resident of the ground floor, between 1950-1954, the legendary jazz saxophonist, often nicknamed 'Bird' or 'Yardbird' was a highly influential soloist and an icon of the hipster subculture.

Born in 1920, in Kansas, he was a virtuoso who introduced revolutionary rhythmic and harmonic ideas into jazz, such as rapid passing chords, new variants of altered chords, and chord substitution.

He died, aged just 34, in a suite of Stanhope Hotel in 1955.

10. Royale

Voted the best burger in NYC, this hidden gem caters to a mix of long-time residents and aspiring young artists from the surrounding Alphabet City.

F. Alphabet City

Creatively getting its name from avenues A, B, C and D which are the only Avenues in Manhattan to contain single letter names.

The neighbourhood has long hosted Manhattan's German, Polish, Hispanic, and immigrants of Jewish descent.

Notable residences have included Luis Guzman, The Strokes, Bruce Willis, Rosario Dawson, John Leguizamo and Madonna.

Founded by Samuel B. Ruggles in 1831, Gramercy Park (above) was once a swamp but now a popular open space, that includes at statue of Edwin Booth in the centre. Union Square Park (below) gets its name from the union of the two main thoroughfares of Manhattan Island – Broadway and Fourth Avenue.

The Penny Farthing (above) became a symbol of the late Victorian era, despite its relatively short use. Its popularity also coincided with the birth of cycling as a sport. It was a dangerous method of travel, but its strengths outweighed the risks at the time. Named the Rover Safety Bicycle, J. K. Starley's modern bike (below) quickly replaced its predecessor.

Fig. 2. Bicycle (Hochrad) von 1880.   Fig. 3. Rover (Niederrad) von 1886.

Matty Maher (above) joined McSorley's as a bartender in 1964, before working his way up to eventually become its manager, and then proprietor. He was manager at the time of the losing gender discrimination case in 1970 that forced McSorley's to remove the last two words of its famous slogan - "Good Ale, Raw Onions, and No Ladies". During its 150-year celebrations Matty hosted NYPD commissioner Raymond W. Kelly and Mayor Michael Bloomberg (below).

A preserved salt marsh on Long Island (above) is similar to ecosystem that exited in the Alphabet City area before its urbanization in the 1820s. Painted in 2018, by Eduardo Kobra, the colourful Michael Jackson Tribute (below) has been a source of controversy since the subsequent resurfacing of allegations in the documentary Leaving Neverland.

Lenox Hill to Upper East Side

Skirting the edge of Central Park, this route visits one of the most iconic city Hotels from a bygone era, before navigating the urban developments that have consumed the once wooded area of Jones Wood Forest.

Recognised as one of the best places in the city to grab a burger, celebrity-haunt JG Melon is on busy Third Avenue.

If it is a chilly day then wrap up warm, as the wind through the buildings from East River can be chilling.

Be aware that Bemelmans Bar is quite exclusive and resides within the hotel.

Start at 68 St-Hunter College Subway

1. Bedford Falls   1:00pm
   206 E 67th Street, NY 10065

2. JG Melon   1:45pm
   1291 3rd Avenue, NY 10021

3. Bemelmans Bar   2:30pm
   35 E 76th Street, NY 10075

4. Luke's Bar & Grill   3:30pm
   1394 3rd Avenue, NY 10075

5. Dylan Murphy's   4:00pm
   1453 3rd Avenue, NY 10028

6. Caledonia Bar   4:45pm
   1609 2nd Avenue, NY 10028

7. Ryan's Daughter   5:30pm
   350 E 85th Street, NY 10028

8. Bailey's Corner Pub   6:00pm
   1607 York Avenue, NY 10028

9. The Five Lamps   6:45pm
   1586 York Avenue, NY 10028

10. Jones Wood Foundry   7:30pm
    401 E 76th Street, NY 10021

11. The Stumble Inn   8:30pm
    1454 2nd Avenue, NY 10021

12. Doc Watson's   9:30pm
    1490 2nd Avenue, NY 10075

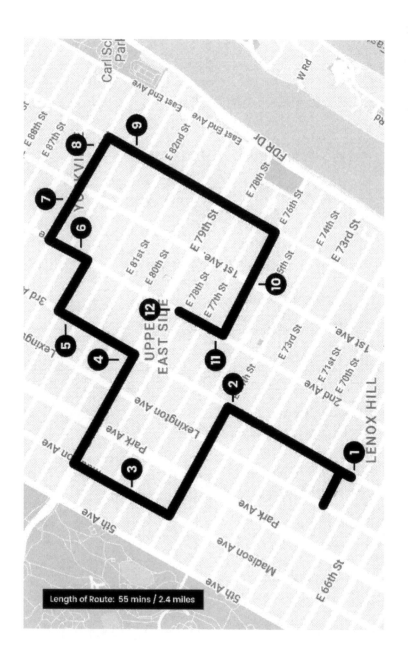

Length of Route: 55 mins / 2.4 miles

Directions

Leave the station and head away from the park, along with the traffic flow, down East 68th Street, taking a first right on 3rd Avenue where **Bedford Falls (1)** is just down East 67th Street over the road. Head back to 3rd avenue **(A)** and turn right where **JG Melon (2)** is a few blocks down on the corner of East 74th Street.

Head towards the park, against the traffic, down East 74th Street, until turning right **(B)** at Madison Avenue **(C)** where The Carlyle is on the corner of East 76th Street and **Bemelmans Bar (3)** within the hotel.

Continue along Madison Avenue, turning right along East 79th Street **(D)**, where **Luke's Bar & Grill (4)** is left onto 3rd Avenue. Follow the road a few blocks, where **Dylan Murphy's (5)** is on the other side of the road.

Turn right from the pub, and take the first left where **Caledonian Bar (6)** is just a few doors down on 2nd Avenue. Continue along 2nd before crossing and turning down East 85th Street where **Ryan's Daughter (7)** is on the right and **Bailey's Corner (8)** on the corner of the following block.

Turn right, down York Avenue, where **The Five Lamps (9)** is on the other side of the road on the following block.

Continue south along York Avenue, before turning right onto East 76th Street, where **Jones Wood Foundry (10)** is at the corner of the block, with **The Stumble Inn (11)** at the end of the next block on the same road.

Leave the pub and turn right up 2nd Avenue, and **Doc Watson's (12)** is a couple of blocks up on the same side of the road.

1. Bedford Falls

This neighbourhood bar shares its name with the fictional town in Philip Van Doren Stern's 1943 short story – The Greatest Gift – that was adapted into, what is considered one of the greatest films of all time, *It's a wonderful life*.

After visiting the mill town of Seneca Falls, in 1945, director Frank Capra found inspiration in its Victorian architecture, central grassy main street and toll bridges.

Like the fictional town, Seneca Falls was home to a significantly rich businessman, Norman J. Gould, who wielded significant control over the local politics and economics of the area.

The fictional town's name is an amalgamation of both Seneca Falls and, the Westchester County hamlet, Bedford Hills.

A. Upper East Side

Before it was the Upper East Side, Yorkville or Lennox Hill, the area between 66th and 77th streets, was known as Jones Wood.

It was the most densely forested land in Manhattan and was named after the owner, John Jones, who had purchased over 75 acres during the early formation of an independent United States.

By the 19th century, it boasted attractions such as bowling, billiards and donkey rides, alongside beer gardens, sporting events and other large public gatherings.

In 1853, it was one of two areas of open space cited in state legislature as possible locations for 'a great park' to address the recreational needs of the expanding city.

Ultimately it lost out to the other option, which became Central Park, and was deemed more suitable due to its convenient location.

Although it remained popular, an 1894 fire destroyed eleven acres and signalled the beginning of a demise that was accelerated by the emergence of the more sophisticated entertainments of Coney Island – which had become more accessible to day trippers with opening of Brooklyn Bridge.

2. JG Melon

Established in 1972, by Jack O'Neill and George Mourges (the J&G in the name), this corner bar is well known for its award-winning Hamburgers.

Previously called Central Tavern, the building dates back to 1920's when it was used by a local brewery during Prohibition.

Decorated throughout with Watermelons, the venue is notable for being the location of a scene featuring Meryl Streep and Dustin Hoffman in Kramer vs Kramer.

Amongst the names hailing its burgers are former Mayor Michael Bloomberg, Food Network Host Bobby Flay, Model Gigi Hadid and actor Dylan McDermott.

B. Madison Avenue Presbyterian Church

The current building was constructed in 1901, when the Eleventh Presbyterian Church (later named Memorial Presbyterian Church in 1872) moved in.

Its first minister, Henry Sloane Coffin, was one of the most famous in the United States. Featured on the cover of Time

Magazine in the 1926, he was heir to the fortune of the furniture firm of W. and J. Sloane & Co.

He was succeeded by George Buttrick who officiated the marriage of Donald Trump's parents, Fred and Mary Anne, in 1936.

C. Madison Avenue

Now carrying traffic uptown, the avenue was not originally featured in the 1811 Commissioners Plan of the Manhattan Street Grid.

Running from Madison Square, at 23rd Street, its name arises from the square which itself is named after the 4th President of the United States.

Since the 1920's, the street's name has been metonymous with the American advertising industry and it has served as the backdrop for the television drama Mad Men, which focuses on the industry during the 1960s.

3. Bemelmans Bar

Based in The Carlyle, the city's premier luxury hotel, the bar, which was opened in 1947, became a popular gathering place for celebrities, politicians and socialites.

Notable patrons have included John F. Kennedy, Judy Collins, Frank Sinatra, Britney Spears, Paul McCartney, Tom Cruise, Robert De Niro and Kim Basinger amongst many others.

It is most famous for the artwork, titled Central Park, that decorates its walls. The pale-yellow artwork depicts children's character Madeline and her eleven classmates.

Already an established artist for The New Yorker, Vogue and Town & Country and with phenomenal success with the Madeline children's books series Ludwig Bemelmans's murals transformed the bar with whimsical scenes of animals in nearby Central Park.

In return for the artwork, Bemelmans enjoyed eighteen months of accommodation at the hotel for him and his family.

D. The New York Society Library

Founded in 1754 as a subscription library, it is the oldest cultural institution in the city, and the de facto Library of Congress during the period when New York was the nations capital.

It was also the city's main library until the construction of The New York Public Library in 1895.

The library moved to its current location in 1937, having grown its collection to over 150,000 titles.

7. Ryan's Daughter

There has been a local club on this spot since before prohibition, with names that varied from 'Old Steam' to the 'Minstrel Boy,' before the current owners transformed it to its current name.

The bar shares its name with the 1970 romantic drama set during WWI in Country Derry, Ireland.

Starring Sarah Miles and Robert Mitchum, the film tells the tale of a married Irish woman who has an affair with a

British officer, despite moral and political opposition from her nationalist neighbours.

10. Jones Wood Foundry

Featuring a sign made by the Fullers Brewery, it is the only one, other than one in Finland, that is outside the UK.

Its wooden building at the back is the oldest one that is not listed for protection in the city.

The main building was constructed sometime between 1875 and 1885 with the commercial floors dedicated to a hardware and plumbing business.

Alongside the business, a foundry produced railings, staircases, lamp posts and manhole covers amongst many others to cater for the city's growing cast iron requirements.

Although the most recognisable, Central Park (above) is only the 6th largest in New York City, covering an area of 843 acres. It is the most visited urban park in the US. Billionaires' Row (below) is the name given to a growing group of luxury skyscrapers to the South of the Park. Several are considered supertall (over 300m) and are categorised as Pencil Towers due to their narrow width.

Designed by architects Sylvan Bien and Harry M. Prince, and built by Moses Ginsberg, the iconic Carlyle Hotel (above) opened, 1930, as an apartment hotel, with apartments which would eventually come to cost up to $1m a year. Its famous Bemelmans Bar is decorated with murals depicting Madeline in Central Park painted by Ludwig Bemelmans.

Situated in New York's East River, Roosevelt Island (above) runs from the equivalent of East 46th to 85th Streets on Manhattan Island - about 2 miles long. Although directly under the Queensborough Bridge it is no longer accessible and, as much of the island is car-free, it is commonly accessed via an arial tramway (below).

Based to the East of Lenox Hill, on the banks of East River, Rockefeller University (above) primarily focuses on the biological and medical sciences and is the oldest biomedical research institute in the United States. The last remain plot of the once vast Jones Wood (below) is hidden and tucked away between a dozen 1870's townhouses, nestled between 65th and 66th Streets and Lexington and Third Avenue.

Bloomingdales to Empire State

This route heads past iconic locations, from Bloomingdales, via the UN Headquarters and embassies of Turtle Bay through to the Empire State Building.

Traversing the city via some of the most memorable and popular locations - The Chrysler Building, Grand Central Station and the New York Public Library - there are fascinating landmarks all through the journey.

Ending in the shadow of the Empire State Building, it is easy to head back in to Times Square or to jump on the Subway home.

Strangelove is everything you would hope to experience for a proper dive bar in the US and not one to miss.

Start at 59 Street Subway

1. Blooms Tavern   1:00pm
    208 E 58th Street, NY 10022

2. P.J. Clarkes   1:30pm
    915 3rd Avenue, NY 10022

3. Draught 55   2:15pm
    245 E 55th Street, NY 10022

4. Stangelove Bar   3:00pm
    229 E 53rd Street, NY 10022

5. Parnell's   3:45pm
    350 E 53rd Street #1, NY 10022

6. The Perfect Pint   5:00pm
    203 E 45th Street, NY 10017

7. Bierhaus   5:45pm
    712 3rd Ave, NY 10017

8. Stout   6:30pm
    60 E 41st Street, NY 10017

9. Blaggard's Pub   7:30pm
    8 W 38th Street, NY 10018

10. Peter Dillon's 36th   8:30pm
    2 E 36th Street, NY 10016

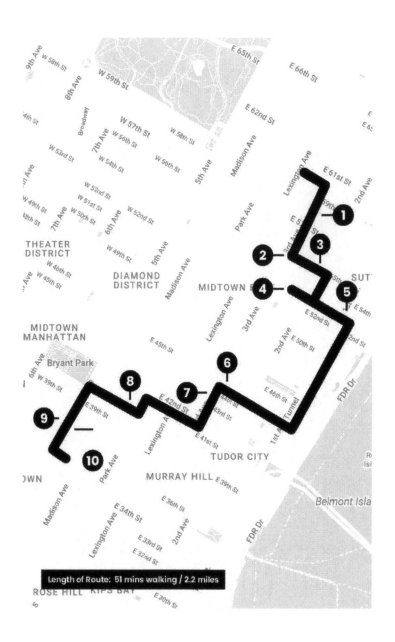

Length of Route: 51 mins walking / 2.2 miles

Directions

Exit the subway, past Bloomingdales **(A)**, taking a right on 3rd Avenue where **Bloom's Tavern (1)** is left, just down East 58th Street. Head backdown 3rd Avenue, where **P. J. Clarke's (2, B)** is on the corner a couple of blocks down.

Turn left from the pub, down East 55th Street and **Draught 55 (3)** is a the end of the block on the same side of the road.

Turning right, down 2nd Avenue, **Strangelove Bar (4)** is right down East 53rd Street. Return to, and cross, 2nd Avenue to find **Parnell's (5)** on the corner at the end of the block.

Turn right, along 1st Avenue, past the United Nations HQ **(C, D)**, and turn onto East 45th Street **(E)** where **The Perfect Pint (6)** is on the corner at 3rd Avenue and **Bierhaus (7)** is opposite on the next block South.

Turn right from the pub, and turn onto East 42nd Street, past the Chrysler Building **(F)**, before turning left into the pedestrian area immediately after passing under the Grand Central Station **(G, H)** flyover.

Turn right onto East 41st Street, and **Stout (8)** is on this block **(I)**, before continuing past the pub all the way to the Public Library **(J)** and turning left at 5th Avenue **(K)**. After turning right onto West 38th Street, **Blaggard's Pub (9)** is on the left, and **Peter Dillon's 36th (10)** a couple of blocks further down **(L)** on East 36th Street.

A. Bloomingdales

With a total of 36 department stores, by far the most famous, is this flagship store that has featured in many films.

Founded in New York City, in 1861, by father and son combo Benajmin and Lyman Bloomingdale, the store grew to occupy most of the block by 1902, before eventually acquiring it all by 1927.

Already a publicly listed business, it suffered from severe financial uncertainty during the 1929, Black Tuesday, stock market crash. Its merger with Federated stores helped it navigate the Great Depression before the post WWII economic boom.

Alongside its Paris fashion and Italian home furnishing catalogue, it was the first US retailer to sell product from Communist China, in 1971.

Over recent years it has opened a further 23 outlet stores in locations such as Dubai and Kuwait.

1. Bloom's Tavern

The character Leopold Bloom's Dublin adventures were made legend as the hero of James Joyce's literary classic 'Ulysses.'

It is almost 100 years since his fictional feats, and yet his notoriety lives on, in this taverns name.

The son of a Hungarian Jew and an Irish Protestant, Bloom famously challenged himself to cross Dublin city without passing a single pub – something that years later still proves impossible.

2. P. J. Clarke's

One of the oldest saloons in the city, established in 1884, stands as a holdout – a smaller, older building not absorbed by an adjacent and larger construction – alongside the 47-story Skyscraper 919 Third Avenue.

The bar has hosted several notable diners over the years including Nat King Cole, who claimed they served him 'the Cadillac of Burgers.'

In 1958, musician Buddy Holly proposed to Maria Santiago here, and a framed photo of their wedding kiss is displayed above table #53.

B. 919 Third Avenue

This otherwise unremarkable looking 47-storey skyscraper was built in 1971 and was part of one of the most unusual real estate transactions in Manhattan.

When the owners of the adjacent P. J. Clarkes refused to sell to developers, they signed a 99-year lease before selling their interest to a consortium led by notorious Ponzi Scheme criminal, Bernie Madof.

C. United Nations

The UN was created after WWII with the aim of establishing peace and as a successor to The League of Nations.

Although headquartered in New York, the organisation has offices in Geneva, Vienna and Nairobi alongside The Hague – which also houses the International Court of Justice.

During WWII, Winston Churchill and Franklin Roosevelt had drafted the Atlantic Charter, with Roosevelt coining the term 'United Nations.'

The initial 'Big Four' countries, underpinning the initiative, were the US, UK, China and, the then, Soviet Union.

Although focused on peacekeeping, during the mid to late 20th-century, the organisation was often paralysed by the Cold War conflict between its two major founding members.

The headquarters, in the Turtle Bay area, were completed in 1952 and houses the General Assembly and Security Council. They are on technically extraterritorial land; however, it acknowledges local laws in return for police and acknowledges fire protection.

D. Dag Hammarskjöld Plaza

Opposite the UN headquarters, this park is named after the former Secretary-General of the United Nations, who held the position between 1953 and 1961.

The economists father served as Prime Minister of Sweden and he remains the youngest person to hold the UN position at just 47 years old.

After his death, in a plane crash, he was posthumously awarded the Nobel Peace Prize – the only decreased recipient of the award.

Given its proximity to the UN building, it is frequently the meeting place and location for protests and demonstrations.

E. Turtle Bay

Due to the proximity of the UN Headquarters, the Turtle Bay district is host to numerous diplomatic missions and consulates.

It is names after a cove on the East River, and was initially farmland for Dutch settlers before becoming a site of slaughterhouses and power plates during the 19th century.

F. Chrysler Building

Formerly the worlds tallest building, for 11 months following its 1930 completion, at 1,046 feet it remains the tallest brick building in the world.

Constructed by the head of the Chrysler Corporation, Walter Chrysler, it was synonymous with the race to build the world's tallest building – in competition with The Empire State Building and 40 Wall Street.

In the style of a gothic cathedral, there are around 50 metal ornaments on the corners of five floors, with the gargoyles represented by vehicle designs and motifs.

On the 31st floor, large hood ornaments resembling the styles of Chrysler vehicles at the time are prominent alongside a grey and white frieze of hubcaps and fenders.

Although prominent on the New York skyline and featured in dozens of films, it was denied an iconic appearance in King Kong as The Empire State Building was selected for the central role ahead of it.

G. Grand Central Terminal

This iconic station is the second busiest in the US, with fellow NYC station Penn Station the only one busier, and serves a staggering 67 million passengers each year.

Opened in 1913, like many of the New York landmarks constructed around that time, its distinctive Beaux-Arts architecture incorporates many works of art.

Part of its name comes from the New York Central Railroad and, although officially Grand Central Terminal, it is most affectionately known as Grand Central Station.

Alongside running a busy terminal that sees a train arrive every 58 seconds, it is amongst the world's top 10 most visited tourist destinations with over 20 million visitors (not including rail and subway passengers.

Its 44 platforms mean it has more than any other train station in the world and has a total of 67 tracks, with the others being used to move or store trains.

H. One Vanderbilt

Construction on this supertall skyscraper began in 2017 and was completed ahead of schedule, before opening was delayed to 2020 due to the covid-pandemic.

It contains an observation deck, above the 73rd floor, that is covered with floor to ceiling mirrors and windows, included mirrors floors and ceilings creating an infinity mirror high above the city.

It takes its name from its location, which in turn is named after the famous family who made their fortune in shipping and railroads during, what was known as, the Gilded Age.

I. Library Way

The series of plaques along 41st Street is known as Library Way and feature quotes from notable authors and poets on bronze plaques embedded into the sidewalk.

There are a total of 96 plaques, duplicated on each side of the road leading up to the Main Branch of the New York Public Library.

J. New York Public Library

The fourth largest library in the world, with around 55 million items, still pales in size to The Library of Congress (175 million) and The British Library (200 million).

Despite several branches across the boroughs, and wider metropolitan area, it is most recognisable for its main branch is the Stephen A. Schwarzman Building on Fifth Avenue, with its impressive entrance flanked by two lion statues names Patience and Fortitude.

The building opened to the public in 1911, several years after the formation of the public library – in 1928 – and was the largest marble structure in the US at that time.

The huge main reading room extends 297 feet long with a 52ft high ceiling, with tables either side of the hall seating up to 490. Unusually there are no columns throughout the room, meaning a wire mesh is installed to support the ornate ceiling.

Surprisingly the library is not funded by government statute and instead is largely supported by private money or philanthropy. Originally created after the US's first multi-millionaire, John Jacob Astor, bequeathed $400k in his will to create a public library.

Other notable donors include industrialist Andrew Carnegie, who donated the modern-day equivalent of $183m, New York Governor Samuel J. Tilden, who donated the equivalent of $78m) and Private Equity CEO, Stephen A. Schwarzman, who underwrote the 2011 restoration with $100m.

K. Stavros Niarchos Foundation Library

More commonly known as the Mid-Manhattan Library, this branch opened in 1970 to house the circulating collection from the Main Branch diagonally opposite.

After closing for renovations between 2017-2020, it was renamed after the foundation that funded the work with a $55m donation – set up to honour the Greek shipping magnate who was one of the world's largest transporters of oil and, at the time, owner of the world's largest super tanker fleet.

L. Tiffany and Company Building

Built as the flagship store of the famous jewellery company, it was completed in 1905, at a cost of $600k.

After the company survived the economic downturn of the Great Depression, it moved to new headquarters along 57th street, the building was occupied by The American Red Cross and Allied Stores, before being purchased by Sun Myung Moon of the Unification Church and turned into offices to publish its daily newspapers.

Its unusual high ceilings means that its seven stories are actually the equivalent of an 11-story structures.

The company that the building gets its name from, known colloquially as 'Tiffany's,' is best known for its luxury goods and diamond jewellery.

Founded in 1837, as 'Tiffany, Young & Ellis', the store initially sold a range of stationery and bric-a-brac items.

Unlike common practice, they were known to mark all items clearly with a price to avoid haggling and refused to accept credit.

In 1879 they purchased one of the world's largest yellow diamonds, which has only ever been worn by four people.

Their insignia design, embossed on a police medal of honour, was adopted by the New York Yankees as their official logo in 1909.

Chief protagonist of Ulysses, Leopold Bloom, as drawn by author James Joyce (above). He was an advertising agent whose Dublin encounters mirrored those of Ulysses in Homer's epic poem – The Odyssey. Viewed from the East River, the United Nations HQ (below) is sometimes referred to as 'Turtle Bay' due to its location.

Although met with mixed reviews initially, the Chrysler Building's Art Deco crown and spire (above) has become a paragon of the architectural style and a notable landmark on the NYC Skyline.

Seen in 1944, Grand Central Terminal is wrapped by a viaduct (above), built to keep traffic moving on 42nd Street and Park Avenue. New York Public Library features in the disaster movie The Day After Tomorrow (below, bottom)

One of the largest yellow diamonds ever discovered (above) has only been worn by four women in its lifetime – Mary Whitehouse, Audrey Hepburn, Lady Gaga (below) and Beyonce – and is estimated to be worth over $25m.

Best of the Rest

Whilst this book has focused on the rich variety of pubs and bars in the Manhattan area there are several bars and neighbourhoods worth exploring that I will look to include in future books.

For now, I have provided some further details of the interesting places you can visit should you find yourself in The Bronx, Brooklyn, Queens or Staten Island.

Sunny's Bar, 253 Conover Street, Brooklyn

There has been a bar on this site since around 1890 and a dive bar exterior masks what is a delightfully run, and well preserver tavern, laced with knickknacks and memorabilia inside.

Montero's, 73 Atlantic Avenue, Brooklyn

This old sailor bar from the 1930's is infamous for its rowdy karaoke nights and its nautical theme, being close to the waterfront.

Dumbo Station, Manhattan Bridge, Brooklyn

This tiny bar is tucked under Manhattan Bridge and is only open in the warmer months of the year.

Evil Twin Brewing, 43 Main Street, Brooklyn

The Danish Gypsy Brewing company – they work with other breweries to produce their either limited edition or one-off beers – first moved to the US in 2019 and has a large selection of craft beers on tap.

Brooklyn Inn, 148 Hoyt St, Brooklyn

The oldest pub in Brooklyn dates back to 1870 and showcases a magnificent carved-wood bar, that was imported from Germany

Yankee Tavern, 72 E 161 Street, Bronx

The oldest sports bar in the Bronx, is a block away from the Yankee's Stadium and has been here since 1927. Legend has it that it was the preferred destination for players Lou Gehrig, Yogi Berra, and Babe Ruth.

Neir's Tavern, 87-48 78th Street, Queens

Operating since 1829, it is one of the oldest bars in the entire United States. At various times in its history, it has featured a ballroom, accommodation and a bowling alley

Bohemian Hall & Beer Grdn, 24th Ave, Queens

One of the largest outdoor venues in the city, it opened in 1910, not long after the influx on Austro-Hungarian immigrants, into Astoria, during the 1890's.

Liedy's Shore Inn, 748 Richmond, Staten Island

Opened in 1905, this is the oldest bar on Staten Island with a salon style bar and a tin ceiling. The walls are adorned with photos of deceased police officers and firefighters who were regulars at the pub.

It is a family-owned pub, founded by the current owners German immigrant grandparents and has been a watering hole for Titanic survivors.

Killmeyer's, 4254 Arthur Kill Rd, Staten Island

Whilst legend has it that parts of the building have been present since 1700's the building became a tavern around 1890 when a mahogany bar was installed. It's been known by several names include 'Rubes' and 'Century Inn'.

Drinking Games

Beer Pong

This drinking game involves players throwing a ping pong ball across a table with the intent of landing it in a cup of beer on the other end.

Typically consisting of opposing teams of two or more players per side, up to 10 cups are set up in a triangle formation at each end.

When a ball lands in it, and stays in it - the contents of the cup are consumed by the other team and the cup is removed from the table. The first team to eliminate all the opponent's cups is the winner.

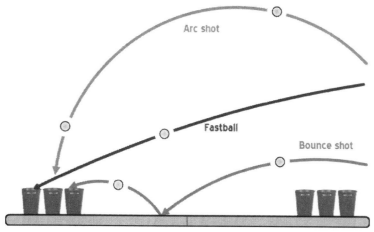

There is a variety of shot techniques, with the most preferred being the arc shot. Depending on house rules, which may remove a toppled cup, the Fastball may be more common.

Typically, the best cups are 18-US-fluid-ounce plastic cups (such as iconic red Solo cups) with the ridge-lines being used to measure the amount of liquid to be poured into the cup.

The game is believed to have evolved from the original beer pong played with paddles which had its origins within the fraternities of Dartmouth College sometime in the 1950s and 1960s.

King's Cup

Played with cards have predetermined drink rules prior to the game's beginning, it is common for groups to establish house rules with their own game variations.

As the game starts, a deck of cards is shuffled and dealt into a circle around either an empty cup or a full drink of choice.

Players assign an action to each card, which is then performed by the relevant person (or players) when it is drawn. Players take turns drawing cards and participating in each assigned category.

Some examples include:

3 – 'Three is for me' – The player drawing the card drinks.
7 – '7th Heaven' –The last person to raise their hands drinks.
King – 'King's Cup' -The contents of the drawers' drink is poured into the central cup and drank by whomever draws the 4th and final King Card.

Paranoia

Usually played with shots, rather than beer, this game requires at least three people around a table.

The first player whispers a *'who'* question into the ear of the person on their right. For example, *'Who has the worst job here?'*

The person who is asked the question says out loud the name of the person they think is the answer.

That person who is named, no matter where they are on the table, can either find out the question that caused them to be the answer or they can play on and ask a new question.

Their forfeit, if they want to find out the question, is to drink an agreed amount - either a shot or a few fingers or seconds of something weaker like beer or cider.

It is of course more fun the more outrageous the questions get, such as *'Who is the worst in bed?'* or *'who has the smallest penis?'*

The game doesn't end but often descends into chaos as the paranoia becomes too much for some people before they call it quits.

Jokes

A fisherman from New York reeled in a 250-pound catfish that was 6'6" long.
Honestly, I don't get the big deal. I do this every day on Tinder.

Where do eggs go on vacation?
New Yolk.

I just returned from a trip in Germany, and I realized just how awful American children are. Sure, they may be nice where I live in New York but kids in Germany are kinder.

When cows go on vacation, where do they go?
Moo York.

What prevented Jesus from being born in New York?
No one could find three wise men or a virgin.

Did you hear that NYC paid Hillary Clinton $2,000,000 as a consultant for New Years Eve?
They wanted an expert on dropping the ball at the last second.

What did the angry pepperoni say?
You wanna pizza me?

Where's the best place to charge your phone in NYC?
Battery Park.

Can a kid jump higher than the Statue of Liberty?
Of course, silly. The Statue of Liberty can't jump.

A woman walks into a bank in NYC before going on vacation and asks for a $5,000 loan.

The banker asks, *'Okay, miss, is there anything you would like to use as collateral?'*

The woman says, *'Yes, of course. I'll use my Rolls Royce.'*

The banker, stunned, asks, *'A $250,000 Rolls Royce? Really?'*

The woman is completely positive and hands over the keys, as the bankers and loan officers laugh at her. They check her credentials, make sure she is the owner and, when everything checks out, they park it in their underground garage for two weeks.

When she comes back, she pays off the $5,000 loan as well as the $45.41 interest.

The loan officer says, *'Miss, we are very appreciative of your business with us, but I have one question. We looked you up and found out that you are a multi-millionaire. Why would you want to borrow $5,000?'*

The woman replies, *'Where else in New York City can I park my car for two weeks for only $45.41 and expect it to be there when I return?'*

Where did the math teacher like to hang out in New York?
Times Square

Have you heard about the new Broadway show based on the dictionary?
It's a play on words.

Where do dogs like to go in New York?
Central Bark.

What is the tallest building in New York?
The New York Public Library—it has the most stories.

I moved to New York City for my health.
I'm paranoid, and it was the only place where my fears were justified.

New York is the city that never sleeps, which is why it looks like hell in the morning.

Why are New Yorkers so depressed.
Because the light at the end of the tunnel is New Jersey.

Think New Yorkers don't get along? I just saw two complete strangers share a cab...
One took the wheels and tires, the other took the battery and the radio.

Random Facts

- A rooster was the first living creature to cross the Brooklyn Bridge

- 21 elephants walked across the Brooklyn Bridge in 1884, to prove to the public that it was safe

- NYC's iconic yellow cabs were once red and green

- The Brooklyn Bridge is three years older than London's Tower Bridge

- It is illegal to have a puppet show in your window

- The New York Public Library is home to over 50m books

- The Statue of Liberty was sent to NYC in 350 pieces

- Albert Einstein's eyeballs are kept inside a safety deposit box in New York

- The Empire State Building gets hit by lightning 23 times a year

- Times Square was named after the New York Times who had offices there

- New Yorkers bite 10 times more people than sharks do worldwide each year

- New York City is home to the largest population of Jewish people outside of Israel

- It would take you 24 hours to travel the length of the NYC subway

- NYC's oldest building dates to 1642, when the Dutch settlers first arrived

- New York City was the first capital of the United States

Rogues Gallery

Acknowledgements

This book does not exist without the internet and the hours of painstaking research that was avoided thanks to the internet and some good friends on the ground.

Our generation carries the entirety of humankind's knowledge in a tiny device in our pocket. I am grateful for the opportunity to provide my small contribution in compiling this list away from our many distractions to provide a little fun, with friends, over a few beers.

Thanks, of course, to my loving family – a wife who has been on almost every pub crawl and my children who make getting up the following day, with a hangover, worthwhile.

Oh, and thanks to Michael for drinking so much over the years that he could share some great suggestions.

How to get involved

Since my first publication, in Autumn 2023, I launched across social media, using the handle @historicpubcrawls and began to revisit all the pubs across my books.

It is great to meet and spend time with the landlords and staff, re-discover some of the areas, continually improve the details in these books and sample exciting new beers.

The best part about sharing the journey on social media has been all the suggestions for new routes and pubs to explore.

If you are not already following me then please do, and join in, by scanning the QR code below, as I love to hear about where I've missed or should be going to next as we start to explore the wider NYC neighbourhoods in the future.

Notes

Visit: www.historicpubcrawls.city

About the Author

Thomas has been running a pub crawl for his birthday almost every year since his mid-twenties.

He has worked in Technology, plays guitar and likes Tattoos, crazy trousers and yellow shoes.

He lives in North West London with his wife, their two sons and their cat Charles Jupiter Whose Eye is an Ever-Raging Storm.

Printed in Great Britain
by Amazon